GUIDING
YOUR
EMOTIONS

Understanding Feelings, Managing Emotions,
Overcoming Negativity and Building Resilience
through Emotional Intelligence

By Inner Balance Books

Table of Contents

Introduction

Emotional intelligence (EQ) is all about connecting with others, handling your emotions, and keeping cool when life heats up. It is also how you keep calm when the pressure is on and get through social situations that would otherwise floor you. Understanding what emotional intelligence comprises is crucial to getting the best out of it.

It's about understanding why you feel happy, and then suddenly, frustration kicks in. It's about understanding your feelings and those of others and why you might feel down, but you tell everyone else you're fine.

In short, life is about emotions, and emotional intelligence helps you take in the emotional data around you and process it. Getting a handle on emotional intelligence helps you work with others, not just at work but in your personal life. Learning to understand emotions is an ongoing skill; there is always room for improvement.

Having high emotional intelligence means you can do the following better:

- Understand your own emotions
- Control them better
- Understand how other people are feeling

- Respond to their emotion in the right way

So, what does emotional intelligence comprise?

Quite a lot, actually, and you need to understand everything to improve yours.

- **Self-Awareness:** Good emotional intelligence is all about identifying and understanding your feelings and why you react in a specific way. Being self-aware means understanding your different moods and responding in the right way, which means better decision-making.

- **Self-Regulation:** This is how you calm your nervous system when your emotions are running high. It's how you stop anger or impulsive behavior from taking over and it's about you managing your emotions, not letting them manage you.

- **Motivation:** This inner voice makes you want to get up and get on with your day, even when you are struggling. Motivation gives you purpose and focus and stops you from throwing in the towel.

- **Empathy:** Empathy helps you understand other people's emotions, helping you connect with them better. Empathetic people are good listeners and understand other people.

- **Social Skills:** These skills are how you make connections and build relationships. Social skills help you communicate, get on with other people, and sort out problems.

Benefits of Managing Your Emotions

Controlling your emotions means identifying your emotions, regulating them, and responding in the right way. You also have a certain amount of control over your reactions.

Emotional control isn't just about managing negative emotions, though. It's about positive emotions, too, although it is far more important to learn to control negative emotions and emotional outbursts that can cause problems.

Everyone experiences a wide range of emotions, and everyone has a trigger that sends them spiraling. It could be something someone says or does, or in some cases, what wasn't said or done.

At the time, your reaction probably makes perfect sense – to you, anyway. It might seem like you seriously overreacted or got things wrong to others. Being able to regulate your emotions helps you become a better person, and it also brings several other benefits:

1. **Better Decision-Making:** Emotional regulation allows you to understand your feelings, control them, and make better decisions. You don't need to let things spiral out of control; you can make an intentional decision and not let your emotions take over.

2. **Making Healthy Choices:** Everyone is guilty of making the wrong choices, especially when they are down. For example, you might choose to smoke, have an alcoholic drink, or eat something unhealthy when your emotions are not regulated. These may make you feel better at that moment but it won't last. Emotional regulation helps you make better, less emotional choices.

3. **Better Communication:** Some people lash out when their emotions get the better of them, which is dangerous. Screaming and yelling is one way but that's not all there is to this. Emotional dysregulation also means that you might not communicate your own needs, making you feel worse in just about every aspect of your life. Emotional regulation helps you listen to your emotions and convey the right message.

4. **Peaceful Relationships:** This directly follows on from communication. When you control your emotions, you communicate peacefully. You can let the other person know that you understand them and are less likely to make sarcastic comments, especially when it feels as though they don't understand you. Emotional regulation can change a relationship's dynamics, be it personal, family, or work.

5. **Self-Confidence:** No doubt that little voice in your head has sometimes told you that you are not important or that you're not good enough. It may make you feel like you don't fit in, but you must learn not to listen. Emotional regulation makes it easier for

you to understand your truths and understand that you have your own strengths and values. In short, it gives you more self-confidence.

6. **More Satisfaction:** This seems obvious – when you make better, intentional decisions, your sense of satisfaction increases. You are more confident and happier, and your relationships are thriving – which applies to work and personal life.

7. **Better Mood:** When your emotions are regulated, your lows are fewer and not as low. And when your mood dips, you can come back from it quicker.

Common Misconceptions

Most people don't talk about emotions – it's a taboo subject! Most conversations revolve around things you've done or your thoughts. It's no mistake that most conversations begin with the words "I think" and not "I feel." Much of this is down to a lack of education about emotion. You are expected to learn how to deal with things by watching others, and if your childhood wasn't filled with great role models, it's no wonder you struggle now.

There are lots of misconceptions about feelings, and these are some of the common ones:

1. **You Should Feel Differently:** How often have you said, "I shouldn't feel like this?" Or "I should be happy to be here?" Emotions don't have rules and there is nothing wrong with

feeling that way. Learn to understand and accept that emotion and that you have a choice about your reactions.

2. **You Have No Control Over Your Feelings:** Your emotions may not be the wrong ones, but there's nothing to say you have to stay stuck in that mood. You can make a choice – you can change how you feel about something by changing how you behave and think.

3. **You'll Feel Better if You Vent:** So many people believe that not talking about your feelings means you are suppressing them and should let them out to make you feel better. In fact, research kicks this into touch, especially in terms of anger. Venting your anger will only make you feel worse about things, not better.

4. **Controlling Your Emotions Makes You Feel Like a Robot:** Too many people believe that emotional regulation means not having any feelings, but that couldn't be more wrong. While everyone can experience many different emotions, they don't have to be controlled by them. Choosing to kick a bad mood into touch and make yourself feel better is healthy, and it's a skill everyone should learn.

5. **Others Can Make You Feel Specific Emotions:** How often have you said, "My boss makes me feel small" or "My parents make me feel bad about myself?" There is no truth to this – no one can make you feel an emotion. Yes, they can influence you, but only you can decide which emotion is right.

6. **You Say You Cannot Handle Certain Emotions:** Some people believe they don't have the capacity for certain emotions, especially those that make them feel uncomfortable. Those people are more likely to practice avoidance. Let's say you struggle to handle confrontation. In that case, you may avoid meeting with someone to resolve an issue you have. Facing difficult emotions head-on makes you more confident, and it's important not to let your emotions control how you behave. You'll learn that you can handle so much more than you thought.

7. **It's Bad to Have Negative Emotions:** Everyone makes the mistake of saying an emotion is good or bad, but the feelings that cause those emotions don't have to be categorized the same. What counts is how you deal with the emotion. For example, anger is considered bad, and some people make poor choices in the heat of the moment. Others use their anger in a better way, making them more productive and not negatively affecting others.

8. **It's Weak to Show Emotion:** In certain situations, not showing emotion is healthy, but for the most part, showing emotions is a sign of strength. However, it only becomes a strength when you understand your emotions and decide to share them rather than letting them take control of you.

Understanding your emotions is not easy, especially when you have always let them control you and never give your feelings a second thought. It takes practice to learn emotion regulation, and this book will give you all the tools you need to get to a place where you finally have full control over your emotions.

If you are ready to begin one of the most enlightening journeys you will ever take, turn the page, and let's get started.

ONE

Understanding Emotion

Emotions. Your whole life is filled with them, and they all influence your life and your interactions with others. Sometimes, you probably feel as though your emotions control you. Everything you do, your choices, and how you perceive situations and other people is influenced by how you feel at the time.

What Are Emotions?

Emotions fall into several categories, and six basic emotions have been identified:

- Happiness
- Sadness
- Disgust
- Fear
- Surprise
- Anger

A person will rarely feel just one emotion at a time. Usually, two or more combine to produce a certain feeling in the same way that you can mix two or more colors to make a different one. Basic emotions are the building blocks that blend to create more complex emotions.

Let's look at those basic emotions and how they impact your life:

Happiness:

This is the one emotion most people want to feel all the time. Defined as a pleasant state where a person feels joy, contentment, and satisfaction, happiness can be expressed in several ways:

- **Facial Expressions:** Smiling
- **Body Language:** A relaxed posture
- **Voice:** Pleasant and upbeat

Happiness may be a basic emotion, but it comes under the heavy influence of things like pop culture, i.e., buying a new car or house and earning a good salary. It's also strongly believed that a link exists between health and happiness. Happier people tend to live longer and have satisfying relationships, while unhappy people tend to be unhealthier and have poor relationships. Unhappiness also leads to stress, loneliness, depression, and anxiety, and that has been linked to a lower life expectancy, inflammation, and a poor immune response.

Sadness:

Sadness is usually characterized by certain feelings, such as a low mood, hopelessness, grief, and disappointment, not to mention a lack of interest in anything. Everyone feels sad at some time, some more than others, and some experience it for long periods. There are several ways people express sadness:

- Low mood
- Quietness
- Withdrawal
- Crying
- Lethargy

When people experience deep sadness, they may turn to unhealthy mechanisms to help them cope, such as pushing everyone away, self-medicating, and focusing only on negativity. These behaviors only make the situation worse and prolong their sadness.

Fear:

This is one of the more powerful basic emotions and is critical to survival. Fear comes into play when a person faces danger, activating the fight or flight response that determines if you run or stay and fight. This is usually characterized by increased respiration and heart rate, tense muscles, and a heightened sense of alertness. This response primes you to deal with threats effectively, and fear may be expressed in several ways:

- **Facial Expressions:** Pulling the chin back and widening the eyes
- **Body Language:** Fleeing or hiding from the threat
- **Physiological:** Rapid heartbeat and shallow, short breaths.

Some people are less sensitive and won't experience the same reactions, but those sensitive to fear may find themselves triggered by certain things.

Fear isn't just about facing a physical threat. Some people suffer from social anxiety, a fear of being involved in social situations. Other people actively seek situations that can bring fear, such as extreme sports, thriving on the adrenaline rush.

Exposure therapy is often used for sensitive people, as gradual exposure to their fears can eventually desensitize them and reduce their reactions.

Disgust:

Disgust can be expressed in several ways, such as:

- **Body Language:** Physically turning away
- **Facial Expressions:** Curling your lip up and wrinkling your nose
- **Physical:** Retching or actually vomiting

Many things can cause this revulsion, such as sight, smell, or taste. It was thought that humans evolved this reaction to detect and keep them safe from harmful, potentially deadly foods. You know how you react when you smell or taste food that has gone off; that's disgust.

Other things that can trigger this emotion are serious infection, bad hygiene, blood, rot, and, in some people, death. It is merely how your body reacts and saves you from something that could potentially harm you.

Of course, there's also moral disgust, a feeling some people experience when they see others doing or saying things they find reprehensible, immoral, or just plain evil.

Anger:

Anger is another powerful emotion where people feel frustrated, agitated, hostile, and antagonistic, usually toward another person. It also brings your fight-or-flight response into play. When faced with a threat that makes you angry, you might decide to face the danger and fight it off to protect yourself. That anger can manifest in several ways:

- **Facial Expressions:** Glaring or frowning
- **Body Language:** Turning away or taking on a strong posture
- **Voice:** Yelling or gruff speaking
- **Physiological:** Reddening or sweating
- **Aggressive Behavior:** Throwing things, kicking, or hitting out

Anger is often considered negative, but it can actually be a positive emotion in some situations. For example, anger can bring clarity in a relationship or help you take the right action to solve a problem.

However, when anger is expressed often, or in harmful or unhealthy ways, it becomes a problem and, left uncontrolled, can soon turn to violence or abuse.

Anger can affect you physically and mentally. Unchecked, it can interfere with your ability to think rationally and can even lead to diabetes and heart disease. It has also been linked to smoking, excessive drinking, aggressive driving, and other activities that affect your health.

Surprise:

Surprise tends to be the briefest emotion and usually happens when a person is startled when something unexpected happens. It can be neutral, negative, or positive and can be brought on by any number of situations. For example, if someone jumped out at you and scared you, it would be an unpleasant surprise. It could be a nice surprise if you got home from work to find all the housework done and dinner on the table.

Some of the things that characterize surprise are:

- **Facial Expressions:** Widened eyes, raised brows, opened mouth
- **Verbal:** Gasping, screaming, or yelling
- **Physical:** Jumping back, throwing your arms up

Surprise also affects your fight-or-flight response, and people can experience an adrenaline burst that helps them prepare to flee or fight.

Other Types of Emotions

Those are just a few of the many emotions humans experience. However, there are plenty of other emotions, including:

- Amusement
- Contempt
- Contentment
- Embarrassment

- Excitement

- Guilt

- Pride in achievement

- Relief

- Satisfaction

- Shame

Emotions are important to humans, as they directly influence your interactions with others, your decisions, and how you behave in certain situations. When you understand those emotions, you can better understand how they come across and affect your behavior.

The Role of Emotions in Human Experience

Emotions play a crucial role in your actions and thoughts. How you feel on any given day directly impacts how you react to a situation or the decisions you make, small or big.

Some emotions don't last long – surprise, for example – while others last much longer, like depression or grief. But why do we have emotions, and what do they do for us?

Where Do Emotions Come From?

The limbic system in the human brain is a series of structures connected to one another, which directly influences your emotions. The important structures are the amygdala, hippocampus, hypothalamus, and limbic cortex, each playing a critical role in your emotions and responses to situations.

Emotions can be broken down into three primary components; understanding those is the best way to understand emotions because each plays its own role.

The three components are:

1. **Subjective:** How an emotion is experienced

2. **Physiological:** Your body's reaction to the emotion

3. **Expressive:** Your behavioral response

Let's look into the role emotions play in the human experience.

- **Motivation to Act:** When faced with a situation that makes you anxious, such as an important exam or interview, your anxiety can make you act, i.e., study harder to succeed. That emotion – anxiety – motivated you to do something positive. Some people will also do things so their emotions are positive, and there is less chance of a negative emotion. For example, you might choose a certain hobby that makes you happy, while you will avoid doing something that will lead to feelings of sadness or boredom.

  Emotions help you take action. Anger makes you likely to confront an irritation, fear will likely make you flee and keep yourself safe, while love leads to happiness.

- **Avoid Danger:** Charles Darwin believed emotions were an adaptation that helped animals and humans survive. They are a way of telling the body it needs to act in a certain way, and emotional responses, such as fear, are usually triggered by the amygdala. Fear can kickstart the fight-or-flight response in your body, resulting in several physiological responses that determine whether you will stay or run. In short, emotions help you act in a way that helps you survive.

- **Make Decisions:** Emotions directly influence your decisions, be it as simple as deciding what to eat or something more complex, like deciding to end a relationship. Research has shown that people with specific brain damage affecting their emotional responses may struggle to make decisions. Emotions have played their part even when you believe your decision has been made through rationality and logic. For example, when you feel fear, your risk perception is heightened. When you feel disgust, you are more likely to throw things away; when you feel angry or joyful, you are more likely to take positive action.

- **Others Better Understand You:** People need to understand your feelings, so when you interact with others, you typically give off emotion via your body language, tone of voice, facial expressions, etc. Sometimes, you may even decide to tell someone how you are feeling, giving them the information they need to do something.

- **You Can Better Understand Others:** Conversely, you can tell how another person is feeling by their emotional expressions, allowing you to promote the right response and build better relationships. It also helps you communicate better in different situations.

Types of Emotions

For most therapists, feelings are cliché, but for a good reason. Feelings play an important role in your life, but most people spend too little time understanding them.

The human body is designed to feel things in response to situations and environments. Sometimes, you won't even be aware of your emotions, but they are always there, driving your behavior and thoughts. The more you understand your emotions, the easier you will find it to acknowledge them, and the more in tune you will be with the world. That will lead to better processing and management of those emotions.

Primary vs. Secondary Emotions

Primary emotions last for less time than secondary emotions but tend to have a more pronounced effect on facial expressions, body language, and physiological reactions. They are more of an initial, instinctive reaction until logic kicks in and the brain begins to process the situation.

Primary reactions include:

- **Happiness:** Pleasure, joy, or contentment
- **Sadness:** Unhappiness, grief, or sorrow
- **Fear:** Terror, dread, or apprehension, usually triggered by potential threat
- **Disgust:** A strong feeling of disapproval or revulsion, usually triggered by an offensive or unpleasant event

- **Surprise:** Shock or astonishment, usually caused by something unexpected

- **Anger:** Hostility or annoyance

Once the logical brain kicks in, your feelings can change quickly, leading to secondary emotions. These last longer and are far more complex than primary emotions, usually learned throughout your life. These secondary emotions can vary significantly from person to person and require much more processing.

Secondary emotions include:

- **Shame:** Distress or humiliation, usually when you realize you've done something foolish

- **Guilt:** Remorse or responsibility for something you've done wrong or believe you've done wrong

- **Pride:** Satisfaction, usually due to a personal achievement or those of people close to you.

- **Embarrassment:** Shame, self-consciousness, or awkwardness, usually experienced in social situations

- **Jealousy:** Usually when you perceive a threat to a possession or relationship you hold dear, and normally felt with anger or fear

- **Gratitude:** Appreciation and thankfulness for generous or kind acts

How to Distinguish Between Them

So, how do you tell if you are feeling a primary or secondary emotion? First, consider the timing of the emotion. What is your first emotion when you face an event, conversation, or other situation? If it's a strong emotion that appeared suddenly and didn't last long, it's a primary emotion. If the emotion hangs about long after the initial situation has passed, it is likely to be a secondary emotion.

Primary emotions are usually borne of instinct, but secondary emotions are usually something you've learned. Secondary emotions are usually all about your feelings about the primary emotion; sometimes, those feelings will provide conflicting information on how to relate to the primary emotion.

Certain role models in your life will instill those secondary emotions in you, and that includes the media and culture. For example, some cultures consider expressing emotions like grief or sadness in public as taboo and shameful. However, given time and effort, you can change that.

Positive and Negative Emotions

We know more than we realize about emotions, which is unsurprising given the research over the years. The most surprising thing is that we don't understand why positive and negative emotions are as important as one another.

- **Positive:** Most people find positive emotions nice. They are considered pleasant responses to anything, be it the environment, a situation, an event, or anything that makes us happy.

- **Negative:** Conversely, negative emotions are unpleasant to experience, usually a negative response to something.

If you experience an emotion that makes you feel weary or down, it's most likely negative.

So, what are these positive and negative emotions? Like any definition, it will depend on who answers the questions. That said, intuition plays a part in helping you determine which one you are feeling. Here are some examples:

Positive:

- Amusement
- Awe
- Contentment
- Happiness
- Interest
- Joy
- Love
- Satisfaction
- Serenity

Negative:

- Anger

- Annoyance

- Disgust

- Fear

- Loneliness

- Melancholy

- Rage

- Sadness

Why do we need both in our lives?

Look at the lists above. How many of those negative emotions do you want to experience? None? That's not surprising. Now, do the same with the positive emotions. But this time, think about a time when you did experience a positive emotion but wished you hadn't. This would normally happen at a time when you don't believe you should be feeling anything positive. Overall, though, most people want to feel positive emotions.

Positive emotions are necessary for people to thrive and function. So, why would you need negative emotions, too? Simply because negative emotions are also necessary for a happy, healthy life, and there are two important reasons why.

1. They are a strong counterpoint. Think about it; if you didn't feel negative emotions, would the positive ones still feel the same?

2. They help you evolve, providing a survival mechanism and a way to develop.

There is a good reason why we experience basic emotions, even the negative ones:

- **Anger:** It helps you fight against issues
- **Fear:** It protects against danger
- **Anticipation:** It lets you plan and look forward to things
- **Surprise:** It lets you focus on something new
- **Joy:** It reminds you what's important in life
- **Sadness:** It helps you connect with loved ones
- **Trust:** It helps you connect with people who can help
- **Disgust:** It helps you reject unhealthy things

Think about it. If you never felt fear, you might not even be here today! A lack of fear could lead to you doing incredibly risky and potentially dangerous things. A lack of disgust could lead to you consuming something harmful. Negative emotions may seem unpleasant, but they are important to your everyday survival.

TWO

The Importance of Emotional Awareness

Have you ever been so busy with life that you forget about your feelings? Emotional awareness is the art of understanding your emotions and it's the most important part of how you interact with others, making logical, rational decisions, and personal development. This chapter will walk you through why emotional awareness is so important and provide you with some helpful techniques.

What Is Emotional Awareness?

Psychology defines emotional awareness as *"the conscious understanding and acknowledgment of your and other people's emotions."* When you are emotionally aware, you will:

- Know when you feel any emotion

- Give that emotion the right label to describe it, i.e., sadness, happiness, anger, etc.

- Understand what caused the emotion and its consequences

- Express it in the right way to yourself and other people

- Regulate it where appropriate

How Does Emotional Awareness Work?

While it might seem like an abstract concept, emotional awareness is a fully functioning, biological process in the brain's limbic system. Let's put it into simple terms:

- **The Initial Response:** When something happens, your senses send data to the amygdala. This part of the brain processes your emotions and kickstarts the initial response.

- **Identifying the Emotion:** The prefrontal cortex controls your behavior and decision-making process. It comes into play here to help you identify your emotions and label them appropriately.

- **Managing Your Emotions:** It takes practice and awareness, but you can learn how to manage reactions to certain emotions, helped by activities and exercises that improve your emotional awareness.

Recognizing Your Emotions

You can't possibly understand how to manage emotions if you don't know how to recognize them in the first place. Some people actively choose to ignore their emotions, but this only leads to more emotions piling up inside them. This denial is purely down to not having enough self-knowledge and not having the ability to use your emotions for the right reasons. Some people struggle to regulate emotions, especially strong ones, and often feel like their emotions control them. This is just as bad a place to be as choosing to ignore them because, in both situations, you will not be able to recognize those emotions, and you certainly won't be able to manage them.

Effective use of your emotions requires you to slow things down. Your emotional process needs to be slowed, giving you the space you need to work out what's going on. Once you can do that, you can begin to understand what's going on, leading to better decision-making in the long run.

Techniques for Identifying Emotions

To recognize your emotions, you must be 100% honest with yourself. If you find it scary to admit what's behind your emotions, you won't be able to work out how to progress. You need to remember that honesty frees you up to make better choices and step away from your old way of reacting. And let's be honest; that old way probably caused you many problems.

Here are the steps to help you identify your emotions:

1. What Happened?

Think about what caused the emotion. Describe it as fully as you can, but fact only – do not use your interpretations.

2. Why Did It Happen?

Think about what could have or did cause the emotional situation. This is an important step because your reaction to something is often down to what you saw as its meaning. For example, you and a friend were planning an afternoon out but they canceled just as you were about to leave the house. How you interpret that cancellation will directly affect your response. Here are two ways you could interpret the cancellation; think about what your response would be for each one:

- She isn't a good friend because she always has other things to do.

- She had an important project due at work tomorrow, so she is likely working on it tonight to get it finished.

Each of those scenarios should elicit a completely different emotional response.

3. How Did You Feel, Physically and Emotionally?

Think about the primary and secondary emotions you felt. If you aren't used to identifying these types of emotions, this will be a little difficult at first, but give it a go – it will be worthwhile. Think about how you reacted physically – did you get a tight throat? Feel a little queasy? Note anything you felt.

4. What Did Your Feelings Make You Want to Do?

This will help you identify what urges you felt, and you must be completely honest with yourself. Admitting that some of your urges may not be right isn't always easy because you may want to do or say things you will regret. Emotions can overwhelm you, but when you learn what your urges want you to do, you can compare your actions. Most people don't act on every single urge they have, which is a good thing. If you can learn to control those urges some of the time, you can learn to do it all the time.

5. What Were Your Verbal and Physical Reactions?

This step requires you to identify your actual reaction to an emotion. You may not have responded in the way you should have, but should be honest about how you responded. Any mistakes you make are your learning curve. Did you say something you shouldn't have done? Do something that was out of proportion or not appropriate to the situation? What do you need to change? How can you handle yourself better in the heat of the moment the next time?

6. How Did You Feel After the Event?

This is the last step, and you need to understand how your actions affect you in the long term. How did you feel after the situation ended? For example, if you faced a situation that upset you badly, did you turn to alcohol to try to make you feel better? When you drink too much, especially if you aren't used to it, there are always negative consequences – nausea, hangover, can't get out of bed and struggle to get to work, or saying things you come to regret. Or you could have lashed out at a partner and said some hurtful things. The consequences of that could be your partner withdrawing from you, feelings of guilt, or even the complete breakdown of the relationship.

Learn to observe yourself mindfully the next time emotions take over. Learn to notice those emotions as they happen, but do NOT judge yourself. Go through these steps as often as needed – with each emotional situation, you'll notice that your reactions gradually improve, and you have more control over your response.

The Benefits of Journaling to Process Emotions

One of the best ways to process your emotions is to journal. It's a great way to help you get a handle on your feelings and learn to identify emotions, where they came from, and how to respond to them.

Let's say you are due in a meeting with your employer and want to ask about getting a pay rise. Understandably, you might feel nervous, and journaling can help you understand why. When you work out where that anxiety comes from, you can determine how best to deal with it and how to get the right outcome – for you, anyway.

Journaling can also help you determine exactly what you feel. In time, you will learn to determine if you feel fear or anger. When you can do that, you understand your emotions, and you can take the right steps to manage them appropriately.

Writing down your emotions and what led to them also helps you see what happened more clearly. Read back over your words and you'll better understand how you felt and why you reacted how you did.

Journaling doesn't just help you with processing your emotions. It can also:

- Reduce your anxiety and stress
- Increase your self-awareness
- Improve your mental health
- Improve your mood
- Lead to less overthinking

- Reduce your blood pressure

- Allow you to regulate your emotions better

- Help you feel better overall

- Lessen the chances of negative thinking

- Enable self-discovery

- Help you express your emotions in a healthier manner

- Help you process your emotions better

5 Tips for Effective Emotional Journaling

There's no doubt that emotions are complicated things, but journaling doesn't have to be. You need only a pen and paper and 15 minutes of quiet time.

1. Find Somewhere Quiet

You don't want to be disturbed, especially when writing about your emotions, because journalling can lead to some pretty strong feelings. Find somewhere private and quiet where you won't be disturbed.

2. Set 15 to 20 Minutes Aside

This is an ideal amount of time – you can write a lot in that time – but if this is your first time, start with five minutes. Gradually increase that to what feels right to you. If handwriting is too hard for you, use a journalling app or a laptop to type your words.

3. Don't Censor Anything

The idea behind journaling is to be honest and connect with your emotional side. You won't learn to understand and process your emotions when you leave stuff out or don't write things exactly as they happened. Write down every negative emotion you experienced and look at why you felt that way and how you expressed it.

4. Prompts Can Be Helpful

Journaling prompts are a helpful way of traveling from analysis to feeling. They can unearth memories you thought you'd forgotten, uncovering emotions you might not have known you had. Prompts are only prompts, though, just to help you start. Once you start writing, just let the words flow.

5. Make It a Habit

It doesn't matter whether you do it once a day or once a week. Get into the habit of journaling consistently. It is your commitment to yourself and to your mental and emotional health. Some people prefer to journal as soon as they wake, while others prefer to wait until just before bedtime. How you do it is entirely down to you. Experiment. Try different times and see what works best for you.

10 Emotional Journaling Techniques

Getting into the routine of journaling is one thing. You must also determine what type of emotional journaling is best for you. You can do it in several ways, and each has its own benefit. You don't even need to stop at one; try different methods for different situations.

1. Stream of Consciousness

This is one of the most unique journaling forms that allows you to write all your feelings, thoughts, and sensations as they come into your mind. This method encourages you to be spontaneous and can have the benefit of uncovering emotions you may have hidden away. If you can't think of anything to write, write some nonsense; the more you write, the quicker your mind will get back on track.

2. Reflective

Stop for a few minutes and reflect on something that happened during the day or just about your day in general. Write down everything you felt, thought, and observed. This can help you learn to be more self-aware and get some perspective on things.

3. Prompt-Based

Use prompts to help you. These are simple statements, questions, or suggestions that can help you reflect and are helpful when you struggle to put things into order. However, be aware that prompts can uncover emotions you may not want to feel, but they are a good way of helping you dig deep into your emotional expressions and how you cope and respond.

4. Dialog

Write to your thoughts or emotions, or write to a person. Write your questions and their responses like you were having a face-to-face conversation. This lets you explore and understand your emotions.

5. Visual

This means you should include images, drawings, paintings, or other visuals that help you – these can be your own drawings, or you could cut them from magazines or print them off the internet. You don't even have to use words if you don't want to. Visual journaling can be one of the best ways to identify and process your emotions.

6. Creative

Most people see journaling as non-fiction, but you can use creative techniques, too. Try writing about an experience in the form of a story told about someone else. This can help you see things from the outside and perhaps pick up on things about your emotions you wouldn't otherwise have noticed.

7. Letters

Write a letter to yourself or someone else, talking about your emotions, things you have a problem with, and your desires. This can be cathartic and help you see things more clearly.

8. Mindfulness

Mindfulness and journaling go together well. Before you begin writing, ground yourself, see your emotions without judging them, and then write them down. This can help improve your emotional awareness and self-acceptance skills.

9. Future

Think about a goal you want to achieve or the future you want to live, and write about it. Go into detail, and don't forget to include the experiences and emotions that go with it. This can help you align your actions with what you want to achieve.

10. Gratitude

This type of journaling can help you feel more positive, and you can do it in several ways. Try writing down a list of things that you were grateful for on the day. Alternatively, take one thing you were grateful for and write about it in detail. This can help improve your physical, mental, and emotional health.

Journal Prompts for Emotional Journaling

Journal prompts are an excellent way to help you get started, especially when you are new to journaling and struggling to know how to begin. Here are some that can help you:

- **What emotions do I feel at this minute?**

  (Write down everything you can feel, no matter how small or big they are.)

- **What part of my body can I feel the emotion in?**

  (Think about the physical feelings you get with the emotion and whether you feel it in a certain part of your body.)

- **What was the trigger?**

  (Was it something you thought of, something someone said, a memory?)

- How do I respond to the emotion?

- When did I feel like this before?

- What are my most common emotions?

- How did those emotions affect how I behaved and thought today?

- What is a healthy way to express the emotion?

- What, if anything, could I learn from it?

(Consider anything and everything you could learn about your needs, values, and desires from the emotion.)

- What were some of the times I felt stressed or frustrated today?

- What were some of the times I felt calm or peaceful today?

- What were my responses to negative emotions?

- How can I deal with negative emotions further down the line?

- How can I bring happiness and positivity into my life?

- What can I do to support myself when I feel this emotion?

(Write down some self-care you can give yourself to ground you when this emotion comes calling.)

Understanding Triggers

Most people go through a whole range of emotions every day – disappointment, excitement, happiness, frustration, and so on. Usually, there is a specific event related to each one, and how you respond to the emotion will depend on the circumstances and your frame of mind.

But what triggers these emotions for you? Everyone is different, but it could be down to something that happened, words, a memory, or anything that causes an intense emotion, no matter what mood you are already in. Knowing your personal triggers is important to learning how to deal with them.

How to Identify Your Triggers

Everyone has at least one emotional trigger, although they vary from person to person. It could be memories you wanted to keep locked down, topics that make you uncomfortable, or even actions – yours or another person's.

Some of the most common triggers are:

- Betrayal
- Rejection
- Unfair treatment
- Loss of control/helplessness
- Challenges to your beliefs
- Being ignored or left out
- Feeling unneeded

- Criticism

- Insecurity

- Losing your independence

- Feeling smothered

Learn to Listen to Your Body

One of the most important things to do is pay attention when you experience an emotional response – that's the only way to learn your triggers. Sure, you'll probably recognize when emotion surges through you, but there are also a few physical things to watch out for, mostly associated with anxiety:

- Upset stomach

- Pounding heart

- Sweating

- Dizziness or shaking

Take a Step Back

When you recognize any of these signs, you need to stop. Take a step back, think about what happened, and how you responded to it. Let's say you had a day off work and spent the day cleaning your home. It's sparkling clean, smells great and there's a romantic dinner cooking in the oven. You wait excitedly for your partner to come home and comment on how great it looks. They don't. Instead, they go to the kitchen, make a snack and sit down without a word to you.

You feel disappointed. All your hard work and not a single word. Frustration and anger begin to build in you. Your jaw clenches, your heart pounds, and all you want to do is snap. Do you stop yourself or let your anger out? Think about how you might respond and how you could respond differently.

Trace the Emotion

Think about those feelings of anger and frustration. Try to work out where they came from. Think about other situations that elicited the same response. Does it feel like you were trying to get some approval from your partner? You didn't get it, and that's why you feel angry. Did it send you back to a time when, say, you did a similar thing to get approval from your parents? A time when, no matter what you did, it wasn't right?

Let Your Curiosity Out

You may not immediately see a connection, so you'll need to think harder. Never ignore a strong emotion, and never try to fight it. Get curious about it to try and understand where it came from. Are there any patterns? Compare it to other situations where you felt the same emotions.

Manage Your Emotions in the Moment

When you know your emotional triggers, you might think you can get away with avoiding those triggers. It doesn't work like that. There is no way you can skirt around every hard decision or situation life brings your way, and no matter how hard you try to avoid them, you will face unpleasant emotions.

Instead, prepare yourself to deal with the triggers and the emotions as they arise. Some ways you can do that are:

1. Own Those Feelings

Tell yourself that feeling a certain emotion is absolutely fine – in that moment. Triggers can cause a lot of different emotions, and there's nothing wrong with that. However, you must accept those feelings before you can even think about working through them. If you deny your feelings or push them aside, they'll only get worse; each time they arise, they'll get harder to deal with.

You can also remind yourself of how things have changed but don't judge yourself. Let's say you are sitting quietly at work, reading on your lunch break. A colleague walks up, snatches the book away, and asks you what you are reading. How does that make you feel? Does it take you back to a time when your school friends or family would take your books and hide them from you?

Instead of dwelling on that, acknowledge that things have changed and you are not the same person. It certainly isn't the same kind of situation. You can take control of things and choose how you want to respond.

2. Make Some Space

Sometimes, just walking away from a situation could be the best thing for you. If the situation allows, excuse yourself and leave. This can stop you from doing or saying something that could come back to bite you later on. Once you have that space, try some grounding or breathing exercises to get your emotions back under control – you'll learn some of those later in the book.

You are not avoiding the situation that triggered you. You are simply allowing yourself time to cool down and see things clearly. When you are calmer, you can go back and try to resolve the situation.

3. Have an Open Mind

Most people you meet won't go out of their way to upset you or make you feel bad. In fact, if they say or do something that upsets you, it's more likely to be a result of their emotional triggers or something else going on in their life.

Let's go back to your spotlessly clean house and your partner who never noticed. Maybe something happened at work, or they got some news that preoccupied them and needed a little space before saying anything.

Every person is a bubbling cauldron of emotions, and unless they tell you what's going on, you won't have a clue. And if the person is someone you don't really know, you'll find it even easier to wrongly interpret things. The message here is not to judge and try to see things from their perspective before you jump down their throat.

4. Communication Is Key

If someone else does something that sets off one of your triggers, talking to them could prevent it from happening again. Step back, calm down, and then talk to them using proper communication skills. Instead of shouting and storming off, tell them calmly why they upset you. Sometimes, challenging someone – in the right way – is a good way of practicing your communication skills. Say, for example, that one of your triggers is sarcastic or unkind remarks aimed at you. Instead of getting upset, ask the person what they mean or what's on their mind to make them say something like that.

Long-Term Healing

While short-term coping strategies are great at helping you deal with triggers as they arise, you should look for long-term strategies to help you heal. There's no need to live with those triggers for the rest of your life.

There are a few ways you can deal with what causes your triggers, and the more you do that, the easier they will become to deal with over time.

- Mindfulness

Mindfulness is one of the best ways to learn about paying attention to your feelings in the moment. Regular practice will help you learn self-awareness, helping you become aware of each emotion you feel during the day. When you can recognize your feelings, you can understand what brings them up and learn coping skills.

Mindfulness meditation is very useful in helping you learn to regulate your emotions but all meditation can teach you to focus and find your inner calm, even in the most difficult of situations.

- Identify Toxic Patterns in Your Relationships

Only you can manage your emotions and triggers; no one else. However, other people are wholly responsible for what they do and say, and that's where your triggers may come from.

For example, a friend who you thought was in a stable relationship is actually having an affair. When they told you about it, you let them know that their talking about it made you uncomfortable. You said you didn't want to hear any more about it, but your friend insists on talking about it all the time. No matter how often you tell them not to, they continue. You feel upset, angry, and disappointed, not just because they are cheating but because they keep crossing your red lines.

Someone who starts to push your boundaries and does so intentionally will not stop, regardless of how often you ask them to.

A healthy relationship involves both parties respecting the other's boundaries. If one party can't do that, it's time to end it because it will harm you in the long run.

- Keep an Emotions Journal

Writing your emotions down regularly can help you spot patterns and identify your triggers. It can also help you identify times when you feel more vulnerable. For example, you might keep your emotions under control when your work is being assessed, but when your partner says they want to go out with their mates instead of being with you, it might be a completely different matter.

Learning this can help you change for the better. For example, if your response to your partner is to shut down, which just makes you feel bad, you can learn another way, perhaps talking to your partner instead of shutting them out.

- Get Professional Help

Some people consider seeing a therapist as a sign of weakness, but it is actually the opposite. Not everyone finds it easy to regulate their emotions, and it isn't an easy skill to learn. You might also struggle to work out what triggers you. Sometimes, your response to triggers is deeply embedded, and you might not even realize what you are doing or how your response affects others.

In this case, it may be wise to seek the help of a therapist, a safe place for you to explore your emotions and identify your triggers and their causes. Therapists can also help you learn communication strategies and guide you through your healing with plenty of support.

THREE

The Role of Emotional Intelligence

Emotional intelligence is about how you can recognize your emotions, understand them, and manage them effectively. But it's also about recognizing and understanding the emotions of people around you.

For most people, intelligence is about their cognitive abilities, including:

- Solving problems using logic skills
- Finding it easy to learn new skills
- Having a large vocabulary
- Memorizing information and retaining it

In short, everything they believe makes up their IQ.

Psychologists have recently begun learning more about emotional intelligence and its importance. Indeed, some even believe it is far more important than any IQ score for determining how efficient a person might be at work.

Some parts of emotional intelligence are related to your personality type, and some of it is down to genetics. However, recent research has shown that anyone can learn to improve their emotional intelligence with training and patience and just a few small changes to daily life.

Emotional Intelligence Components

Emotional intelligence can be broken down into five components:

- **Self-Awareness:** Understanding and being aware of your own emotions. A person with high emotional intelligence is well aware of their emotions and can label them in the right way. They also understand how their actions affect others and how emotions can change.

- **Self-Regulation:** Once you have mastered self-awareness, you can begin to learn self-regulation. Being aware of emotions makes it easier to manage them and your responses. It could mean that when you are aware of a hard emotion, you consciously make yourself slow down and resist the temptation to respond inappropriately.

- **Motivation:** This is when you are stimulated to do something and is an important part of emotional intelligence. Motivation keeps you following your goals, no matter how challenging it may be. If a person isn't motivated, they'll fall at the first hurdle and give up. A highly motivated person sees that perseverance is worth the effort and pushes on, no matter the obstacles.

- **Empathy:** This is about how well-tuned you are to other people's emotions. A person with high emotional intelligence is better at identifying other people's emotions and can see the difference between real and fake emotions. This can be down to noticing body language, facial expressions, and changes to their voice.

- **Social Skills:** A more emotionally intelligent person will find it easier to interact with others in the right way. Emotional intelligence is crucial to building and maintaining relationships and communicating appropriately with others.

Why Is Emotional Intelligence So Important?

When you have good emotional intelligence, it helps you work with others and cope with the stresses life throws your way. Research shows that emotional intelligence can improve many areas of your life, including:

- Anything related to work, including management skills and teamwork, and can make a person more satisfied with their job

- Psychological well-being

- Physical health

- Social relationships

Improving your emotional intelligence can also lead to:

- Better stress management

- Better mood

- Better self-expression

- More emotional understanding
- Better emotion management

In short, the higher your emotional intelligence, the happier you are, with more self-confidence better social skills, and the easier you will find it to handle stressful situations.

Conversely, people with low levels of emotional intelligence are more likely to turn to coping mechanisms, such as alcohol and tobacco, to help them manage stress and are also more at risk of eating disorders and self-harming.

Let's look at an example that shows the difference between high and low emotional intelligence.

You were asked to send an email to one of your organization's largest clients. That email was time-sensitive, and you didn't send it. Your manager may be angry and may even worry that they will lose their job.

A manager with low emotional intelligence is likelier to lash out, shout at their team, or deny a problem exists. That could lead to the team becoming discouraged and avoiding responsibility in the future.

A manager with high emotional intelligence would understand their emotions but would also understand that lashing out won't solve the problem. Instead, they choose to engage in calm, supportive talk, building motivation among the workers and trying to resolve the issue.

That manager would exhibit a high level of empathy and would know when to ask questions, what questions to ask, and whether disciplinary action against you was appropriate. They would also know that those conversations shouldn't take place in front of the other team members and shouldn't disrupt things.

Improving Your Emotional Intelligence

It is perfectly possible to improve your emotional intelligence and you can do it in several ways. However, it does take time, effort, and practice. Here are 10 ways you can practice to build your emotional intelligence:

5. **Daily Intentions:** Set an intention each day based on your schedule. For example, you could set the intention to build your understanding of others.

6. **Self-Care:** When you look after yourself and get plenty of rest and relaxation, you can control your emotions better.

7. **Emotional Checkup:** Take the time to think about your feelings and consider your body's reactions to any given emotion.

8. **Slow Down:** Before reacting to or going into a potentially stressful situation, stop and take a breath.

9. **Ask Questions:** Talk to others to understand their emotions better, and you'll find your skills in empathy improve, leading to better emotional intelligence.

10. **Make Space for Your Emotions:** If you can understand and acknowledge negative emotions, you can learn to work on them, and one of the best ways to do this is to practice mindfulness.

11. **Be Aware of Others:** Pay attention to those around you and your environment and learn to recognize other people's emotions. When you are in company, turn off your phone, for example, so you are with your friends and not focusing on your Facebook feed.

12. **Connect with Others:** When you interact with others in a way that shows them you understand them, you'll find it easier to notice their emotions.

13. **Don't Be Afraid to Apologize:** If you make a mistake, admit it. The higher your emotional intelligence, the easier you will find it to be accountable for your actions and take responsibility for them.

14. **Start and End the Day Positively:** Start your day on a positive note – listen to your favorite music, meditate, etc., and end it with gratitude, noting everything you are grateful for that day.

CHAPTER

FOUR

Techniques for Managing Emotions

When something unexpected happens, do you struggle with overwhelming emotions? Do you struggle to get a handle on things? You are not alone. Many people struggle to manage their emotions occasionally, but when you let them take over, and it happens all the time, it can become a problem.

Thankfully, plenty of tools can help you gain and retain control. This chapter walks you through ways to manage your emotions and why self-regulation is so important.

The Importance of Self-Regulation

It's called self-regulation when you can choose your reaction to emotions and feelings. As a child, your relationships with your parents and family help you learn emotional management – it's not something you just know about. You may struggle to manage emotions and self-regulate if you don't grow up in a supportive home or environment.

It's never too late to learn, though, and there are some techniques you can try to help you.

Cognitive Behavioral Techniques (CBT)

The thinking behind CBT is that how you interpret a thought, feeling, or situation is directly related to whether you will experience psychological problems. You are more likely to exhibit unhealthy behavior when you interpret things negatively.

CBT changes your thought processes, and you can eliminate or at least reduce unhealthy behavior by changing how you think and interpret things. CBT can also teach you the strategies and skills you need to handle everything life throws at you.

Getting Started

You can try several CBT techniques to help you change how you respond to emotions. These techniques include breathing exercises, muscle relaxation, behavioral activation, and much more. Let's look into those now.

Self-Monitoring

This is one of the more basic skills and is the basis of virtually every CBT technique listed in this chapter. It's the perfect starting point.

Here's how it works. The only way you can address an issue is to be aware that it exists, and that's where self-monitoring comes in. Once you are aware of the problem, you can begin to regulate your response and behavior to produce a better outcome.

Developing this skill requires you to consciously pay attention to your behaviors, thoughts, and reactions. Journaling can help you identify these. As you become more aware, you will likely start seeing patterns and learn what triggers your response. Journaling can also help you track progress on your journey to better skills.

Diaphragmatic Breathing

Otherwise known as deep breathing, diaphragmatic breathing is another basic skill that can help you cope with situations and manage your anxiety. A simple technique it may be, but it is also one of the most powerful.

It's no more difficult than breathing from your diaphragm while breathing in deeply, and you'll learn how to do it, along with other breathing techniques, later in this chapter.

Progressive Muscle Relaxation

You can use a CBT app to help you with this, as most offer relaxation exercises to help you reduce anxiety. One of the exercises is called PMR – Progressive Muscle Relaxation – and it requires you to switch between relaxing and tensing the different groups of muscles throughout your body.

To go into a state of complete muscle relaxation, you must first do the opposite, tensing every muscle, holding them tense, and then gradually releasing them so your muscles feel relaxed. Muscle tensing is common during bouts of anxiety and stress, and PMR can eventually help your body realize that muscle tension is actually a signal that your muscles should relax.

Behavioral Activation

When you feel anxious or depressed, you are less likely to do anything that makes you happy. That's why you need to learn a CBT skill called behavioral activation to help you get active, even if it's the last thing you feel like doing.

The skill has a simple goal – to become more active in the happier, more enjoyable areas of your life. Your mood will improve when you get involved with these areas and engage with them. As that happens, your behaviors and thoughts follow suit. It's also a good way to take your mind off things, so if you've always enjoyed running, get your running shoes on and hit the trails when you feel anxious.

Writing the Pros and Cons

It isn't always easy to make a decision, let alone the right one, especially if you continually have negative thoughts. Trying to make a decision when you are depressed or anxious can leave you stuck and feeling trapped, and you often won't know which way to turn. You might even make a snap decision that turns out to be completely wrong.

The best way to get past this is to stop and make a list of the pros and cons, short and long-term. This CBT strategy can help you work out the best route to take, i.e., the one that causes the least risk while ensuring you still move forward.

Cognitive Restructuring

Another coping skill, cognitive restructuring is all about changing how you think about others, yourself, and situations. It's about weeding out the negative thoughts and interpretations and changing them.

You will learn to gather information about specific thoughts and understand how you or others could misinterpret them. You will then learn to use positive affirmations in place of those negative thoughts, and by doing so, you will gradually change your thoughts and make better choices.

Goal Setting and Management

Goals are things that you want to do, not necessarily just in the short term. They can give you a sense of direction in life and motivate the behaviors that will help improve your life. However, goals can also take over and cause a lot of stress, so you need to be very careful when you set them.

This skill teaches you to approach goal-setting to help you feel better and have a better quality of life without causing you undue stress and anxiety. This could mean that, rather than setting one large goal, you break it down into smaller goals and give yourself an easier go of things while still achieving what you want.

Sometimes, you need a helping hand. You cannot always cope with every problem that comes up, not alone, and CBT can help you develop the skills needed to handle tough emotions and situations.

Mindfulness and Meditation

When you can put a label on a tough emotion, it can help you unstick yourself from it. The amygdala lessens its activity when you do this, which means a stress reaction is less likely to occur in your body. When you can put a name to an emotion, you can feel its hold on you release, giving you some emotional space. This allows you to recognize the emotion without being overwhelmed by it and gives you space to decide how to respond to it.

Here's a useful mindfulness meditation practice to help you:

1. Find somewhere comfortable to sit, away from distractions. Sit in a chair in an upright position with a relaxed but alert posture. Close your eyes – partially or fully, it's your choice – and breathe in deeply a few times to help your body relax.

2. Become aware of your body. Notice how you are sitting and feel all the sensations in your body at that moment.

3. Put one hand over your heart and feel as you breathe in and out. To make things easier to start with, just focus on breathing in. Rest and wait for the next breath. Repeat for one minute – leave your hand where it is or let it drop into your lap if you like.

4. If something distracts you or your mind wanders away from your breathing, bring it back gently.

5. As you continue to be aware of your breathing, notice the emotions that begin to arise in you. Move your attention from

your breath and ask yourself what you are feeling in that moment. Ask yourself what those emotions are. If you began the meditation with no strong feelings, you might feel contented. You might feel curiosity, yearning, or some other emotion. Focus on it and understand what it is.

6. Give the strongest emotion a label – if two or more emotions are vying for attention, give each one a label. Use your body like a kind of antenna to pick up on the strongest emotion. Name it and repeat that name three times, quietly and gently. Return your focus to your breath and feel each one. Turn back to the emotions and repeat, moving between the two, relaxing more as you do. If a certain emotion starts to overwhelm you, focus on your breath until you feel able to face the emotion again.

7. With your hand over your heart, feel each breath and feel the warmth. Feel the love inside you that made you want to do this exercise. Feel the good within you and keep breathing mindfully. When the emotion tries to take over, label it, sweep it away, and focus on your breath again.

8. Slowly open your eyes and sit for a minute.

Whenever you face a stressful situation or feel a strong emotion arising, you can always turn to your breathing, label your emotions and relax into it. You'll find it much easier to work with and manage.

Breathing Exercises and Grounding Techniques

Grounding is a great technique to help kickstart relaxation in your body. This can bring about a sense of calm and help you focus on the present moment. Here are some grounding exercises to help you get started.

Grounding Through Breath

Your breath is one of the best tools you have at your disposal to help you focus your attention. It only takes a few minutes to help you clear your mind and work through strong emotions, and there are several breathing techniques to choose from.

Box Breathing:

1. Breathe in deeply while slowly counting to four, feeling your lungs filling with air.

2. Hold your breath for a count of four seconds – do not inhale or exhale.

3. Slowly breathe out through your nose or mouth for a slow count of four.

4. Hold your breath for a count of four seconds.

Repeat as many times as it takes.

Diaphragmatic Breathing:

1. Put one hand lightly on your upper chest and place the other just underneath your ribs.

2. Breathe in through your nose slowly, feeling your belly push out. The hand over the chest shouldn't move if possible.

3. Pull in your stomach muscles, pulling your belly in while you purse your lips and breathe out. Again, the hand on your chest should not move.

Repeat as often as needed.

Pursed Lips Breathing

- Let your shoulder and neck muscles relax.
- Breathe in through your nose slowly for a count of two, not opening your mouth.
- Purse your lips and breathe out slowly for a count of four.

Repeat as much as needed.

4-7-8 Breathing

- Keeping your mouth closed, breathe in through your nose for a count of four.
- Hold your breath for a count of seven.
- Open your mouth and breath out, making a 'whoosh' noise for a count of eight.
- Repeat at least three times.

Grounding Through Gentle Movement

Another way to calm yourself is using gentle movement, and there are a few methods to choose from.

Elf-Push

- Position your hands in front of your chest. Your fingers should be pointing down, and your palms pressed together.

- Pull your shoulder blades in and move them down and backward.

- Breathe in and hold the posture, but relax.

- Breathe out, pressing your palms hard together.

- As you do this, imagine the whole movement beginning in your shoulders and back, and mentally note the changes you feel as you do this.

Repeat this exercise three to five times.

Self-Pull

- Position your hands in front of your chest with your index fingers interlocked.

- Pull your shoulder blades down and back.

- Breathe in and hold the position in a relaxed state.

- Breathe out, pulling your interlocked fingers without releasing the clasp.

- As you do this, imagine the movement starting in your back and shoulders and mentally note any changes you feel.

Repeat three to five times.

Squeeze Hug

- Hug yourself by crossing your arms over your chest.
- Hold each upper arm with the opposite hand and pull them in towards your body.
- Squeeze them as you pull them in, using only as much pressure as you are comfortable with – over time, you can increase this.
- If it feels right to you, breathe in and out deeply as you squeeze.
- Continue squeezing for a few minutes, then release gently.

Repeat as often as needed.

Slow Run

- Start by sitting in a chair with your feet flat on the floor.
- Press one of your feet into the ground slowly.
- Release it and repeat with the other foot.
- As you do this, imagine the movement begins in your hip and upper leg.
- Continue doing this for several even deep breaths.
- Speed up or slow down as it suits you, and mentally note all changes you feel as you do it.

Repeat up to three times.

Toe-Heel Breathing

- Start by sitting comfortably.
- As you breathe in, lift up your toes.

- As you breathe out, lower them again.

- Repeat five times.

- Then, breathe in and lift your heels.

- Breathe out and lower them.

- Repeat five times and mentally note any changes you feel.

Grounding Using Your Senses and Self-Talk

You have five senses, and any of them can be used in conjunction with self-talk to help you ground yourself. Your senses can help you release your worries and reduce the impact of strong emotions. While practicing the following techniques, talk to yourself, encouraging yourself as if you were helping a friend.

Butterfly Tapping

- In a comfortable position, cross your arms over your body. Place each hand on the opposite shoulder.

- Tap each shoulder with your hand, taking it in turns to do each side.

- If you don't find this position comfortable, place your hands on opposite thighs or knees and tap those instead.

- As you tap your shoulders or knees, talk to yourself. Use a simple "I" statement, such as "I can do this," "I am okay," or "I am safe."

5-4-3-2-1

- Sit or stand comfortably.

- In your head or aloud, say the following:

- o Five things visible around you

- o Four things you can reach out and touch

- o Three things you can hear

- o Two things you can taste or smell

- o Inhale and exhale once.

Repeat up to three times.

Stress Management Strategies

Everyone gets stressed at times, but some people handle it better than others. If you struggle to handle stress, you need to learn some stress management techniques.

Identifying Your Stressors

You're at work. The phone won't stop ringing, your emails are out of control, and you are struggling to reach an imminent deadline. Your boss is hovering, constantly asking you how things are going. It's no wonder you are stressed.

These situations are short-lived and fall under the term "acute stress." When your workday ends, those stresses should be left behind, and sometimes, a little bit of stress like that is good for you.

However, if this happens every day, and you struggle to leave things behind when you go home for the day, you could have another type of stress, a longer-term type called "chronic stress." Left unchecked, chronic stress is harmful to your physical and mental health.

Some of the biggest stressors people face are changes in their lives, problems at work, money issues, and relationship problems. Smaller stressors include having to travel long distances for work, rushing about in the mornings and having a little too much work and not enough time on a given day. These can also add up and become bigger stressors. Your first step is to recognize what causes the stress in your life. Only then can you begin to manage them.

Let's break the stressors down.

Personal Life

There are six main stressors you may face in your personal life:

1. **Health:** Getting older, getting an unwelcome diagnosis, or complications from a disease you may already have can increase your stress levels. It could even be happening to a friend or family member and your closeness to them will cause stress in your life, too.

2. **Relationships:** When you argue with friends, spouse, family, or even colleagues, it can be stressful, more so when you all share an office or house. And if other household members are having problems that don't directly involve you, it can still cause stress.

3. **Personal Beliefs:** If you have specific personal, political, or religious beliefs that others don't agree with, it can cause problems. It worsens if you are embroiled in a conflict you can't escape. Stress can also arise when something big happens that

makes you question what you always believed in, especially when you and those close to you don't share the same beliefs.

4. **Emotional Problems:** If you struggle to express certain emotions or you find it hard to relate to someone, stress can weigh you down. And if you have depression or anxiety, it just makes things worse. This is why you need to have some positive outlets and, if necessary, professional help to manage your stress.

5. **Life Changes:** A change in job, a new house, or losing someone close to you can all cause stress in your life. Even if the changes are good ones, like getting married, it can still be stressful.

6. **Money:** Money is one of the biggest causes of stress, be it not earning enough to live on, credit card debt, unpaid rent, or anything else related to money. Especially these days, when we live in a world where having "things" seems more important than being able to afford them.

Social Issues

Social issues also cause a great deal of stress in people's lives.

-   **Employment:** Research shows that one of the biggest sources of stress is a high-pressured job or conflict at work.

-   **Discrimination:** If you feel someone discriminates against you, it can cause huge stress. Examples of this include gender, ethnicity, and sexual orientation.

- **Environment:** Stress can arise when you live in a city where crime is high, your neighborhood is unsafe, or you feel unsafe in other ways.

- **Traumatic Situations:** If you have ever experienced a traumatic or life-threatening event, it can cause chronic stress. Examples include war, rape, robbery, or a natural disaster, and in some cases, you could be diagnosed with PTSD – post-traumatic stress disorder.

How to Deal with Stress

You will not go through life without experiencing at least one stressful situation. It could be something small, like getting stuck in traffic, to something much larger, like illness or losing your job. It doesn't matter what causes it; stress causes a hormonal surge through your body, your breathing gets faster, your heart pounds and your muscles tighten up.

Luckily, you can learn some relaxation techniques to help you cope better with stress as it arises.

1. **Breath Focus:** This is simple to learn but incredibly powerful. It involves diaphragmatic breathing, and as you breathe in and out slowly, you must shut your mind down from sensations and thoughts that distract you. This is a helpful technique for those with an eating disorder as it helps them focus on themselves more positively. However, you should not try this if you have a medical condition that makes it hard for you to breathe, such as heart failure or lung disease.

2. **Body Scan:** This combines breath focus and PMR (progressive muscle relaxation.) Breathe deeply for a few minutes, then begin to focus on one muscle group or part of the body and mentally release the tension. Do this for every part of your body, and you'll find it makes you more aware of the connection between your mind and body.

3. **Guided Imagery:** Close your eyes and bring images of experiences, places, or scenes that relax and calm you. There are plenty of free apps to help you here, so long as you only choose calming images. Guided imagery can reinforce a more positive view of yourself, but it may not work for you if you struggle with thoughts constantly intruding.

4. **Mindfulness Meditation:** As mentioned earlier in this chapter, mindfulness meditation is a way of helping you focus on your breath and be in the present moment without your mind becoming distracted. It is a popular technique, and it can help people with stress, depression, and anxiety.

5. **Qigong, Tai Chi, and Yoga:** These are three of the oldest arts and combine flowing movement, relaxed postures, and rhythmic breathing. The physical part allows you mental clarity that helps you clear your mind of distracting and stressful thoughts while making you more balanced and flexible. However, if you are inactive, have a condition that stops you from moving, or have another health condition, you must check with your doctor first, as some of these may be hard for you.

6. **Repetitive Prayer:** This technique is all about repeating a short prayer in your head while you focus on your breath. You could even use a phrase from a prayer if it has a special meaning to you.

Don't just pick one method. Try them all and see what works best for you. You might find that different situations call for a different technique, too. Whatever you choose to do, set aside at least 20 minutes per day. If this is too much for you to begin with, start with five minutes and work your way up, but make sure you do it daily. Consistent, regular practice is the only way for these techniques to truly offer any real benefits in reducing your stress.

CHAPTER

FIVE

Communicating Emotions Effectively

This is one of the longest chapters in the book because effective communication is the key to everything. Good emotional health is crucial to your mental and physical well-being. Whenever you experience something, no matter what it is, an emotional response is generated. If you can talk about it, you'll find it easier to process and regulate your emotions. When you struggle to talk about your feelings, you can't do that, at least not in a safe or healthy way.

The Benefits of Communicating Your Feelings

Communicating your emotions, positive or negative, provides you with plenty of benefits, especially in your personal growth. You become more self-aware and a better communicator, and you'll find it easier to express your emotions without feeling guilty or ashamed. That leads to more self-confidence and an overall better you.

1. **Improved Self-Awareness:** Understanding your emotions isn't always easy, but learning to talk about them can improve that understanding. When you can talk to others, you can look at

your emotions objectively and learn more about your emotional self. If you talk to the right person, they can sometimes offer you insights that you might not be aware of.

2. **Deep Communication:** General conversation is quite shallow – think work conversations, a chat with a neighbor at the bus stop or at the checkout in the local store. That's fine; you don't need to get into deep and meaningful conversations with these people. When it comes to your family and personal relationships, things are different. Talking about your emotions can help you build strong, genuine connections with those who are important to you.

3. **A Genuine You:** If you can't talk about your emotions, people can't hear you and they won't see you for the person you are. If you can talk about your feelings, they see the real you, allowing you to be a better version of yourself. You are also more likely to attract those who resonate with the real you, leading to deeper, better relationships.

4. **Better Decision-Making:** When you become more self-aware, you learn more about yourself, what you want, and the boundaries you need to set. That allows you to make better, more informed decisions.

5. **Less Anxiety and Stress:** If you know you can talk to someone about your feelings without feeling ashamed, it lessens the anxiety and stress that comes with negative situations and

emotions. That leads to you dealing with other potentially emotional events more calmly.

6. **More Self-Confidence:** Being able to express your emotions in a safe and healthy way lets you connect more deeply with the important people in your life. It lowers your stress levels and improves your self-confidence no end.

The Healthy Way to Express Your Emotions

Effective communication is assertive, not aggressive. It requires you to make clear statements about your needs, beliefs, and, more importantly, your emotions. Assertive communication allows you to advocate for yourself politely and honestly and be less judgmental and more considerate of other people's feelings.

Assertive communication is one of the best ways to resolve conflicts healthily and without unnecessary confrontation. It doesn't matter if you need to tell a colleague you can't help them with their work or if there's something you and your life partner need to discuss. Being assertive lets you talk about things productively, and you can work together to resolve the issue.

Here's what assertive communication would look like in certain scenarios.

Conversation with a Friend

A close friend fancies your roommate, and the feelings seem to be reciprocated, at least partly. When you try to make plans to do something with either person, they also want to know if the other person will be invited. That irritates you. You've been here before; the last time a friend and roommate started dating, things got a little uncomfortable and unpleasant. You also know your friend is interested in getting serious, while your roommate only wants a brief fling.

Your friend finally asks you if you would be okay with them dating your roommate. What do you do? You could go all gonzo on them and scream and shout that, no, it wouldn't be okay. Or you could be a little less aggressive and communicate your feelings properly.

You could tell them that you are concerned a relationship between them would get in the way of your friendship. Tell them that something similar already happened to you and how complicated it made things. Tell them you lost a good friend because of it, and then tell them your roommate is only looking for a causal relationship.

Your friend might be disappointed but, if you talk to them in the right way, they won't lose their temper. They may agree with you and not want to hurt your friendship; they may even acknowledge that a relationship could get in the way.

Conversation at Work

For the last week, your boss has been discussing a big upcoming project they want you to work on because you know the client. They tell you it will be a good experience for you and help you get a promotion, which you are totally ready for. When you finally get the project and see the due date, you panic a little. You don't have long and you already have other work you must finish – you can't do everything yourself but don't want to let the client or your boss down. It's time for a talk.

You tell your boss that, while you want to prioritize this project, you don't want the rest of your work to suffer, either. You tell them that you want to do the best job you can.

Your boss agrees that you already have too much work, and you work together to determine what work to shift to another team member, giving you the time you need to do the job.

Conversation with a Partner

You are in a serious relationship, and you love spending time with your new partner, but one thing irritates you – they are really messy! Whenever you go to their home, there's dirty laundry all over the place, dirty dishes on every side, and the bathroom isn't all that clean. You've dropped some subtle hints, but nothing has worked. Rather than saying anything else, you just ask them to come to your place; it's clean, and you feel more comfortable there.

That's all good until they ask you why you don't like visiting their home. You need to be honest, but you don't want to hurt them, so you tell them that messy rooms make you feel stressed and anxious. You ask your partner if they would be willing to tidy up a bit and clean the dishes (and bathroom) before you visit to make you more comfortable.

If you do this right, your partner won't feel like you are jumping down their throat or judging them and they agree to clean up before you visit.

Why Assertive Communication Is Worth It

Assertive communication takes time to learn, especially if you usually respond aggressively or passively. However, it is worth the effort to learn because it brings a ton of benefits:

- **Your Needs Are Protected:** Setting sensible boundaries allows you to have limits on what makes you uncomfortable. Assertive communication lets you express emotions safely and clearly and use them to set your boundaries. By deciding what you will do and, more importantly, won't, you look after yourself and your needs first. If necessary, remind others of your boundaries – that way, you retain control when situations threaten to get out of hand, and it lessens the risk of frustration and resentment.

- **It Helps Build Trust:** You've always been told that it's best to be honest, which means you need to learn assertive communication. If people know you will be honest and open with them, they will trust you. Passive communicators often leave details out or tell small white lies. You may not consider yourself a liar, but omission or vagueness amounts to the same thing. People know when you are being vague with them, making them less likely to trust you. Likewise, aggressive communication can also make people less likely to trust you because you frighten them.

- **It Reduces Stress:** Think about the conversation examples you read, specifically the work-related ones. Rather than just taking on more work, you initiated a conversation about the work you already have. You may well have been able to do all the work, but it wouldn't have been a stress-free situation. Passive communicators do not tell people what they need, and they don't set boundaries and stick to them. This leads to them getting overwhelmed and stressed. Likewise, aggressive communicators are usually stressed. Not many people are happy to work with someone who hides their feelings or needs, and rather than offering support, they will likely leave you to do everything.

- **It Stops Conflicts:** Go back to that conversation with your roommate. What would have been the outcome if you'd been aggressive and told them they simply couldn't date your roommate because it would be bad for you? That would likely have resulted in your friend resenting you and a conflict that could end your friendship. Conversely, you could have answered passively and told them you didn't care what they did. That might not have caused a conflict immediately but if their relationship did end up straining your friendship, your frustration would get worse, ending in an explosion of anger. Annoyance could be at them for the relationship and you for not saying what you felt, which can lead to passive-aggressiveness. You might slam doors when your roommate and friend are in the room or sink to sarcasm. Conflict is less likely to happen when you can assertively state your case.

- **It Increases Self-Confidence:** Assertive communication can make you feel more confident, leading to more satisfying relationships. You'll find it easier to talk to others and build relationships with like-minded people who fully respect your boundaries and needs.

Assertive Communication Techniques

Assertive communication will be difficult to learn if you are naturally passive or aggressive. There are some techniques you can use to teach yourself to start speaking up and protecting your own needs and emotions.

1. **Understand Where the Problem Lies:** People who are vocal around people they know might struggle with new people. Others might be quite aggressive when they feel threatened or involved in a heated conversation. You might be assertive in communicating your feelings to your spouse but not with other people. Or you might be aggressive in your workplace because no one listens otherwise. That's the first step – identifying where you struggle to be assertive.

2. **Recognize Your Feelings:** If you don't know your needs, you can't express them. Self-discovery is a good way to help you understand your needs and emotions. Listen to your internal self every day and ask yourself:
   - What made you feel stressed or anxious?
   - What made you feel good?
   - What did you enjoy?
   - What did you not want to do?

It can also help to learn when you stop yourself from responding instinctively. You might feel like saying the first thing that pops into your head, but that's not always tactful or helpful.

Often, you will develop two skills at the same time: assertive communication and emotional awareness. When your emotional awareness is good, you can recognize when to communicate assertively and when to let something pass.

3. **Ask for What You Want:** Everyone has the right to express their needs but you can also ask others when you need something, be it for them to change how they behave or you need help with something. Sure, they might say no – that's their right – but just starting that conversation respectfully could lead to something good.

4. **Use Your "I" Statements:** Especially when you want to get your feelings across or are asking for something. I-statements are all about you, not other people. If others don't feel like you are judging or blaming them for something, they are more likely to help. For example, your parents need help cleaning the house out. You could say, "I've been really busy this week and need a day to myself. I'm happy to help you clean the house, but can't do it this weekend. How does next weekend work for you?" You'll likely get a better response than if you just give a straightforward, "No, I can't help."

5. **Practice Makes Perfect:** If assertiveness doesn't come naturally to you, try practicing with friends and family first. Learn to be comfortable with asking for help and telling others how you feel. When the time comes for you to face a difficult conversation or situation, you'll find it easier to cope. Ask your friends and family to help you learn when you are being aggressive or passive – that way, you will learn the right way to respond to people.

Troubleshooting

If you are a natural worrier, you might avoid assertive communication, thinking that other people will find you overbearing or selfish. Some people consider an assertive person to be aggressive, usually when they don't know the difference between them. However, you shouldn't avoid using assertive communication in case you upset someone. Here are some tips to help you be more successful:

- **Be Specific:** Saying "No, thank you" is not an aggressive response, and you don't have to add any more. However, a refusal is sometimes better accepted if accompanied by an explanation, especially if you value your relationship with the other person. Let's say your friend asks you to join them for lunch. Instead of just saying no, you could say something like, "Thanks, but no. I'm working through lunch so that I can leave a little earlier tonight." That tells them they haven't done anything to upset you.

- **Watch Body Language:** You'll learn more about this shortly, but communication is about more than the words you say. It's also about body language. Let's say your flatmate consistently forgets to take the trash out when it's their turn. You could respond by folding your arms, taking an aggressive stance, stomping out, and doing it for them while grumbling under your breath. The body language alone tells them you are angry even if your words don't. Instead, calmly remind them it's their turn or ask them if they want to swap chores if it's causing a problem.

- **Ask About Them:** While you must put your own needs first, it doesn't mean ignoring how other people feel. Good communication is a two-way street. When you've stated what you need, consider asking the other person for their thoughts or suggestions. Listen when they talk – don't interrupt.

- **Keep Your Cool:** Emotions are always there, bubbling beneath the surface, and a stressful situation can easily bring them out. However, try calmly telling others how you feel rather than blowing your top and using aggressive body language. Don't forget to use your I-statements. If necessary, use one of the breathing techniques you learned to help you calm your body, or step away for a few minutes until you are in control of your emotions.

While some people confuse assertiveness with aggressiveness, there is a subtle difference, and it's all down to how you say things and your body language. Expressing your feelings is never wrong, so long as you do it tactfully and respectfully.

What Is Body Language?

Body language is an important part of communication. Instead of words, your facial expressions, physical body posture, and mannerisms can speak volumes. Most of the time, body language is instinctive; most people don't do it consciously. You may not be aware of the fact that, when you talk and interact with other people, your body is speaking and sending messages of its own, usually much louder than your words.

Body language can help people decide whether to trust you. It can offend people, undermine your words, or it can tell them that you are someone they can believe in. Even when you don't say anything, your body language does.

Sometimes, your verbal words and body language are at odds with one another. For example, you might be telling someone that you are happy to go along with whatever they say, but your body language – tight posture, crossed arms, etc., - might tell them the opposite. The person you are talking to will notice this and have to decide what to think – which message is the right one, the verbal or the nonverbal? Most people will choose to believe your body language because it rarely lies.

When you understand your own body language, you can learn to express your true feelings and intentions, which will foster better connections with others and better relationships, at work and personal.

Better communication requires understanding body language, not just yours but others.

Different Types of Nonverbal Communication

Nonverbal communication falls into several types:

- **Facial Expressions:** Your face often speaks far more than your voice, displaying many different emotions. The facial expressions for the different emotions, i.e., anger, happiness, sadness, etc., are universal.

- **Posture and Body Movement:** Think about how other people stand, walk, or hold their head or body. Does it change how you see them? Body movement and posture convey a lot of different things that may go against or agree with what you are saying.

- **Gestures:** We make gestures all the time, usually unconsciously. Waving, pointing, and waving your hands around when talking are all gestures, but they may be interpreted differently in other cultures. For example, while the "OK" hand sign is fine in English-speaking countries, it is offensive in others.

- **Eye Contact:** This is one of the most important aspects of nonverbal communication, and how you look at someone speaks volumes. Your eyes can indicate hostility, interest, attraction, and much more. Eye contact also helps keep a conversation flowing and helps you gauge whether the other person is interested in what you say.

- **Touch:** This is another good communication tool – a strong handshake, a warm hug, a pat on the head, etc. These all give their own messages.

- **Space:** How often have you felt someone is standing too close to you, invading your personal space? Everyone needs space, even physical space, although how much differs between people, cultures, and situations. Physical space can say a lot, from being a sign of intimacy to dominance, aggression, or even fear.

- **Voice:** Yes, your voice is a verbal communication tool, but your tone of voice is nonverbal. People listen to how you speak, not just what you say. This includes your pace, timing, loudness, inflection, tone, and other sounds, all playing a role in what you are really saying. The tone of voice can indicate confidence, aggression, anger, sarcasm, and much more.

Can You Fake Nonverbal Communication?

Lots of websites and books claim to tell you how body language can be used to your advantage. They tell you how to sit or how to position your hands to give off an air of dominance or confidence. You can't fake nonverbal communication because you have no control over every signal your body sends. Your body constantly indicates your state of mind and everything you feel, and the more you try to fake it, the harder those signals will come across.

That said, you do have a certain amount of control. For example, let's say someone says something you disagree with. Your body language would typically be negative to disagree with what they say – you might avoid looking at them, cross your arms, or tap your fingers or feet. There's nothing to say that you have to agree with what has been said, but you can consciously stop your body from sending those negative signals. You must learn to keep your stance open and indicate that you want to understand their point of view. When you can see things from the other side, you'll have more luck at getting your body language to talk for you.

When Body Language Goes Wrong

Your nonverbal communications affect what others think of you and whether they respect or trust you. Sadly, nonverbal communication can go wrong when people send negative signals without knowing it. This can damage the connection between you, as you can see from these examples.

Example #1:

Jack thinks he and his work colleagues are good friends and get on well. However, ask his colleagues, and they tell a different story. They find him intimidating. They say his eyes are piercing when he looks at them. He lunges at them to grab their hands and then squeezes hard, hurting them. Behind the scenes, Jack is a nice guy and his only (secret) wish is that he had a few more friends. Sadly, his nonverbal cues speak volumes, and he comes across as awkward. This keeps people away from him, and it is hurting his chances of promotion.

Example #2:

Angie is an attractive young woman who doesn't struggle to meet men but can't seem to keep a relationship going beyond a couple of months.

She is funny, interesting to talk to and always smiling and laughing. Her body language tells a different story. She comes across as tense. Her eyebrows and shoulders are raised, she speaks shrilly and she has a stiff body posture. People don't stay around her long because she makes them feel uncomfortable and anxious. She has so much in her favor, but her body language puts people off.

Example #3:

When Tony and Jackie met, Tony thought he'd found the perfect woman, but Sharon didn't see it that way. Tony works hard, is good-looking, and is a real smooth talker, but he doesn't seem to care about Jackie's thoughts. He's more wrapped up in his own and whenever Jackie expresses her thoughts, he knocks her back before she's even finished talking. She feels like he ignores her, so she starts seeing other men. Tony is also struggling to move on at work for the same reason. People stay away from him because he doesn't listen to anyone else, and although he admires many of them, he is not popular with them.

All three of these are smart people with good intentions who find connecting with others hard. It's all down to their negative body language and sadly, they are mostly unaware of it and have no idea of the effect it has.

One way to build strong relationships and learn effective communication is to understand your body language and use your nonverbal communication more positively.

Improving Your Nonverbal Communication

Nonverbal communication is a constant form of communication that needs your focus. If you are looking at your phone, lost in thought about what you might say or thinking of something else, you'll miss the cues and misinterpret what's going on.

Nonverbal communication can be improved, along with learning to be in the moment, and it can help you improve your stress levels, manage stress when it arises, and improve your emotional awareness. Here are some tips to help you.

1. Learn Stress Management in The Moment

When you are stressed, you can't communicate effectively. You'll misread situations and people, your nonverbal cues will be confusing, and you'll sink into unhealthy behavior patterns.

When stress takes over, you need to step back. Take a few minutes to calm yourself before you rejoin the conversation. Once you have a handle on your emotions, you'll find it easier to deal with the situation positively.

In time, you will learn to do this in the moment, and the easiest way to do that is to use your senses. Think about things you can hear, see, touch, smell, or taste. Or use a movement that soothes you. You could look at a photo of your family or pet, listen to music, or use a stress ball, all of which can help you relax your mind and focus. Experiment to find what works for you because everyone will have different things that relax them.

2. Improve Emotional Awareness

To use the right nonverbal communication, you must be fully aware of your emotions and their influence over you. But that's not all. You also need to be aware of and understand other people's emotions, which comes down to emotional awareness.

When you are emotionally aware, you can:

- Read other people and their emotions accurately and understand their nonverbal signals.

- Send nonverbal signals that back up your verbal communication, creating security and trust in your relationships.

- Respond in a manner that shows people you care about them and understand them.

Most people don't have a good connection with their emotions, particularly the stronger ones, because they were taught to shut their feelings down. Yes, you can deny your feelings, but that doesn't mean they'll go away. Instead, they will just grow stronger and interfere in your life, affecting your responses and behavior.

When you develop emotional awareness, you will find it easier to connect with your emotions, even the unpleasant ones, and better control your actions and thoughts. Mindfulness meditation is an excellent way to help you develop emotional awareness.

3. Learn to Read Body Language

When you have learned to recognize your emotions and manage stress, you'll find it easier to understand nonverbal communication from others. Here's what you need to do:

- **Watch for Inconsistencies:** Verbal and nonverbal communication should always say the same things. Are the person's nonverbal cues saying the same as their words, or do they say the opposite?

- **See All the Nonverbal Signals:** Don't see one cue and read too much into it. You need to consider all the cues you see from another person's body language. Taken as a group, see if you can tell if they say the same as their verbal cues.

- **Trust Your Gut Feelings:** If you feel that someone is lying or not being completely honest, it's likely you are unconsciously picking up on inconsistencies in their nonverbal and verbal communication, even if nothing else looks out of place.

Navigating Difficult Conversations

Difficult conversations are a fact of life. Everyone faces one at some point in their life. It's how you handle those conversations that's important. More than 60% of people lose sleep worrying about how the other person in the conversation will react. One of the biggest reasons many avoid difficult conversations is not to elicit a negative, possibly aggressive reaction.

Nobody likes having these conversations, but there are ways you can prepare to ensure the conversation goes the best it can.

1. Listen

You've got to have this conversation, but it's not one-sided. When the other person is talking, listen to what they are saying. Don't tune out to think about what you might say next. By doing that, you are ignoring what they are saying.

- Listen attentively – your nonverbal cues should tell the other person that's what you are doing, too.

- Try to see things from their perspective. Ask questions that show you want to understand – "Tell me about it," or "Tell me how that made you feel."

- Never talk over them. Always let them have their say.

Doing this could teach you something you didn't know about the person or the situation. The other person will also be able to see that you are fully engaged with them, making the conversation go more smoothly and positively, with less negative emotion. The one thing you never do is enter the conversation thinking you know everything – you don't.

2. Be Clear About Your Feelings and Expectations

Clear and direct communication is one of the most important parts of a difficult conversation. Take some time before the conversation to plan what you need to say to help you keep your emotions under control.

- Get the facts ahead of time. Never go in unprepared, as the conversation will quickly get out of hand.

- Explain how the situation that led to the conversation has made you feel, talk about your thoughts, and why it made you feel that way.

- Use your I-statements. For example, in a conversation with your partner, don't say, "You don't care about me!" Say something like, "I feel upset when (whatever the situation is.) When you use You-statements, the other person likely feels as though you are attacking them, and they'll shut down.

- Discuss what you want the conversation outcome to be. Do you want an apology? An acknowledgment that they understand your perspective? To change how they behave in the future?

Listen to their point of view, too, and it should help provide a clear path through the conversation.

3. Try to See Things from Their Perspective

It's so easy to get caught up in your own feelings that you don't see theirs. This is especially the case if you have something awkward to say or you've been hurt by something they did or said. Before jumping to conclusions, try to see things from their side of the equation. Ask yourself the following questions:

- Can you think of five reasons they might have said or done what they did?

- Have they ever acted like this before? Is this completely out of character for them?

- Is there something in their work or personal life that could indicate their behavior?

- Did you do anything that could have upset the apple cart, so to speak?

People act and say things for all different reasons. It isn't always about you, so try to find out what's going on and see things from their perspective.

4. Take a Break if Needed

Sometimes, it doesn't matter what you do. You won't get anywhere if the other person isn't being constructive or fighting against you at every turn. If emotions have taken over, here's what to do:

- Encourage them to talk about their emotions, but only if you and they feel safe doing so. Sometimes, it helps to get stuff off your chest, and it could be exactly what's needed to solve the problem.

- Walk away. You can try again later when things have calmed down; a break could be just what they need to get their thoughts in order.

- Ask a third party to get involved, so long as they are not close to the situation. This can help cut the tension and help both sides to reach a workable solution.

Sometimes, walking away, if only for a few minutes, is enough to let tensions calm.

5. Agree to Disagree

You won't always reach a happy conclusion. Each person has their own ideas and thoughts, and sometimes you just won't be able to talk through a problem. That's fine. It's not a reflection on you or the other person. You may just need to agree to disagree – it does not mean either of you is right or wrong. It just means you pick your battles and walk away when things can't be resolved.

6. Protect Yourself

Sometimes, a difficult conversation can get emotional, and looking after yourself in this situation is important. Taking some time out is fine, especially if it stops people from saying things they might come to regret. Take the time to go for a walk, listen to your favorite tunes, or talk to other people about things that have no bearing on your conversation – happy things.

If you know someone who has had to have a similar conversation, try talking to them to see if they can offer you some insight and support in handling the situation.

Be proud that you made the effort to have the conversation. It took a lot of courage and each time you have to do something that helps you be less nervous, it will help you build up your confidence and skills. Having difficult conversations will never be easy, but you can lessen the stressful impact on yourself and others.

Strategies for Discussing Emotions with Others

When you hold your emotions inside of you and never express them, you cannot hope to process them, and you'll struggle to handle them. Opening up and letting those emotions out will benefit your health physically, mentally, and emotionally. It can reduce stress levels, strengthen your immune system, and reduce emotional distress.

Many people struggle to talk about emotions. They overthink things, worry that others will judge them, or struggle with finding the right words. There isn't a right way to do it, nor is there a wrong way.

You could seek support from your friends or family, or you might find seeing a therapist easier. Whoever you choose, you must feel as though the person supports you and makes you feel safe.

Here are some tips to help you open up:

1. Comfortable Communication

If you find it hard to speak to someone face to face, try a phone or video call. You could even try writing a letter or sending an email. However you do it, you must be comfortable.

When you write a letter or email, it gives you some space to think about what to say. Journaling is an excellent way of letting your emotions out without having to talk to another person. This can help you get ready for that face-to-face talk about your emotions.

2. Time and Place

When the time is right, you must find a comfortable, quiet place where others won't disturb you. Whoever you plan to talk to, tell them in advance if you can, letting them know you want to talk to them in confidence. That lets them prepare and give you the space you need.

3. Practice

It might sound daft, but knowing what you want to say or how you want to start the conversation can be a big help. Don't overthink things, but do have an idea of what you want to say. Be flexible enough to let the conversation flow as it needs to. If you have a rigid plan, it can cause even more stress, especially if things don't go as you want. You also need to allow the other person to speak – even though these are your emotions, it's still a two-way street. Good ways to open the conversation are things like "I've been finding it hard to cope recently" or "I haven't been feeling so happy recently."

4. Honesty Is the Best Policy

If you want others to understand your feelings, you need to be honest in how you talk about them. You need to be able to tell them how those emotions affect you and how they make you think and act. When you can draw a connection between your emotions and behaviors, it can help others understand things better, not to mention help you see things more clearly. You should also be prepared to talk about other emotions those feelings have brought up, perhaps guilt, anxiety, shame, or even anger.

5. Explain Your Feelings

Tell others how hard it is for you to open up. It allows them the chance to respond helpfully and sensitively. Say something like, "This is hard for me, but I think it would help me to share my feelings." That gives you a little space, too, some time to settle into the conversation. If something makes you uncomfortable, tell the other person and let them respond, giving yourself a little more time and space.

6. Suggest Things That Might Help

It might help if you and the other person discuss examples of things that could be helpful. It could be changes to your job, asking your partner to listen to you more, or anything that helps you alleviate the stress and anxiety your feelings bring.

7. Start Slow

Don't expect to do this in one conversation. It might take several, but that's fine. Your goal is to talk about your feelings and experiences in a way that you and the person you talk to feel comfortable. It isn't down to you how others behave or respond, but it can be good for both of you to have time to process everything and come back to it another time.

In the same way, if the other person says something that upsets you or appears unwilling to help, don't be afraid to walk away and find someone else to talk to – it's kinder to you in the long run. You shouldn't have to convince or beg someone to help you, but you also don't have to justify your feelings. Keep your boundaries in place and find the right person to talk to.

8. Be Open But Independent

When you start to open up about your feelings, you might be tempted to depend on the person you talk to. Don't. The idea is for you to talk about your emotions as a way of helping you manage them; that way, you can be independent and support yourself. By depending on other people, you can't do that.

Some people can help lessen your anxiety, but this should only be used as a way of empowering you to be self-supportive. Talking should give you the strength you need to manage things but also create an open and trusting relationship without making another person feel responsible for your feelings.

9. Show Yourself Kindness

If you start to feel guilty about talking through your emotions, unsure if you are doing the right thing, or uncomfortable, stop. Ask yourself how you would react if the situation were reversed if someone were talking to you about their emotions. What would you say to them? Now, say it to yourself.

Emotions affect your learning ability, creativity, and your ability to develop healthy relationships and keep them. That means finding the right way to explore your emotions and express them. Yes, you will likely feel vulnerable when you talk about your emotions, but it's really a kindness to yourself. With the help of a listening ear, you can find the ways you need to work through things and manage your emotions. At the same time, you also give the other person permission to talk about their feelings. Remember, it's a two-way street, and everyone involved will be happier and healthier for it.

Conflict Resolution Skills

Conflict is normal, it's a part of life and part of every healthy relationship. You can't agree on everything 100% of the time. However, how you deal with the conflict is crucial.

When you deal with it wrongly, conflict has the ability to harm your relationship. Handle it right, and your bond will be stronger for it.

What Is Conflict and What Causes It?

Conflict is not just a disagreement between two people. It can be a situation where you and/or others feel threatened, even if there is no real threat. Ignore it at your peril. Conflicts don't get better with time; they simply get worse until we face them.

Most people's response to a conflict is based solely on how they perceive a situation. It rarely has anything to do with actual facts. These conflicts can cause people to experience strong emotions; if you struggle to handle those, you'll struggle to resolve the problem.

However, you should see them as a way of growing. When you can resolve your issues successfully, your relationship strengthens, and there's more trust and security.

Conflicts can arise from differences of opinion over anything. The difference may be small or seemingly insignificant, but it can trigger strong emotions. In a case like that, the core likely comes from a personal need, be it to feel safe, respected, valued, or for more intimacy.

Think about how a parent and child have different needs. While the child wants to explore and is happy to head to the edge of the street, the parent needs to protect them. That protection can only come by limiting how far the child can go. The parent and child are at odds with one another, causing conflict.

Each party's needs are important to a relationship being successful, and each should be given the right consideration and respect. In a personal relationship, when the two parties don't understand each other's needs, it leads to arguments, a widening gap between them, and a breakup. In the workplace, it could result in deals not getting done, profits falling, and jobs being lost.

Recognizing what has caused the conflict is the first step. The next is being prepared to examine the conflict with understanding and compassion, which leads to stronger relationships and better understanding.

Responding to Conflict

Do you face it or run from it? Fear it? If you have perceived some kind of conflict because of something that happened to you in another relationship, you may be under the impression that every disagreement will end badly. If something happened to you early in life, it could even result in you seeing conflict as traumatizing.

If you already feel threatened or fearful when you enter a conflict, you won't find it easy to deal with healthfully. Instead, you'll explode in anger or shut down completely.

Here's a look at how to respond to conflict:

HEALTHY	UNHEALTHY
Being able to empathize with another's perspective	Not being able to recognize what matters to another and responding to it in the right way
Calm reactions, not defensive, and respectful to the other party	Explosive reactions, hurtful words, anger, and resentment
Forgive and forget mentality, move on and not resent the other party	Withdrawing love, intimacy, and attention and making the other person feel rejected, ashamed, and isolated

Not punishing the other person and seeking a compromise	Not being able to see the other person's side and not looking for a compromise
Believing that facing the conflict is the best way for everyone to deal with it	Fearing the conflict, avoiding it, and expecting a negative outcome

Conflict Resolution, Stress, And Emotions

Strong emotions may be triggered in times of conflict, leaving a person disappointed, hurt, and uncomfortable. Handled wrongly, conflict can leave deep rifts that simply can't be repaired. It can also lead to deep resentment, even relationship breakups. Resolved right, conflict can strengthen relationships, build trust, and help you understand others better.

When you and your feelings are not connected, or your stress levels are so high that you can only focus on one or two emotions, you can't possibly understand what you need. That will make talking to others hard, and you won't be able to tell them the problem. For example, many couples squabble over silly things rather than actually facing the real problem.

To resolve conflict successfully, you must be able to:

- Quickly manage your stress while staying calm. That will enable you to read nonverbal and verbal cues accurately and interpret them.

- Control your emotions and responses. When you can do that, you'll find communicating your needs much easier without resorting to intimidation or threats.

- Pay attention to all feelings, not just your own, not to mention what others say.

- Respect differences. No two people are the same, and respecting other's views and thoughts will make it easier to resolve the conflict.

Quick conflict resolution requires you to learn two skills:

1. Quick Stress Relief

Managing stress in the moment is the only way to remain focused and take control of your emotions, regardless of the situation. You'll soon be overwhelmed and tempted into unhealthy responses if you don't.

Think of driving as a way to describe how people respond when stress takes over:

- **Full Throttle:** The agitated, angry response where you are hot under the collar, wound up and full of emotion, unable to stay still.

- **Hard on the Brake:** The depressed, withdrawn response where you show little to no emotion and shut down.

- **Full Throttle While Braking Hard:** This is a tense response, where you freeze up, unable to do anything. However, underneath, you are bubbling with agitation and emotion.

Stress gets in the way when you want to resolve a conflict, and it stops you from:

- Rasing body language correctly
- Hearing what the other person really says
- Being fully aware of how you feel
- Being in touch with your needs
- Communicating those needs clearly and concisely

Earlier in this chapter, you learned how to reduce stress in the moment – refer to those skills now.

2. Emotional Awareness

As you learned earlier, emotional awareness is about understanding yourself and other people. When you don't understand an emotion or why you feel it, you can't resolve conflicts or communicate properly.

Knowing your feelings might sound simple, but most people push strong emotions aside. How you handle conflict is all down to your connection to your feelings. If you hide from strong ones, you'll struggle to resolve differences with others.

Emotional awareness plays a key role in conflict resolution because it centers around your ability to process and manage your feelings and communicate effectively. It can help you:

- Understand the real problems someone is struggling with

- Understand your own emotions and problems

- Keep your motivation high until you have resolved the issue

- Communicate assertively

- Interest others and, hopefully, influence them into healthy responses and behaviors.

How to Assess Your Emotional Awareness

The quiz below will help you work out your emotional awareness level. For each question, provide one of the following answers:

- Almost Never

- Occasionally

- Often

- Very Often

- Almost Always

There is no right or wrong way; the answers you give are designed to help you develop your awareness of your emotional responses and improve them.

1. Do you/have you ever had feelings that seem to flow from one to another?

2. Do you feel any physical responses when you feel these emotions? In your chest? Stomach?

3. Have you ever had distinct emotions in your facial expressions, i.e., happiness, sadness, anger, etc.?

4. Do you have feelings strong enough that you and other people notice them?

5. Do you notice your emotions? Pay attention to them? Do they play a part in the decisions you make?

If you don't recognize one or more of these experiences, likely, your emotions are off or at least dampened. In that case, you need to work on your emotional awareness, which you learned about in Chapter 2: The Importance of Emotional Awareness.

Nonverbal Communication and Conflict Resolution

Amid a conflict, you need more than just the words people say. You need to look for the nonverbal cues, the signals that say more than verbal communication. This could be facial expressions, gestures, posture and the tone of voice used. Understand those, and you can understand more about the other person and their point of view, allowing you to respond better and really get to the heart of the matter.

Emotional awareness allows you to read other people accurately. The more you connect with your own emotions, the better you can read the nonverbal cues the other person gives off. Think about the words you say and your body language at the same time – do they agree with one another? Or are they telling different stories? For example, if you tell someone you are okay while standing stiffly and not meeting their eyes, it's clear you are not fine – your body language says that. Using a calm voice or the right expression on your face can pay off when trying to resolve a conflict – it can relax the atmosphere and reduce the stress, leading to more chances of a successful resolution that meets everyone's needs.

CHAPTER

SIX

Building Resilience

You've survived a stressful situation, but how do you pull yourself back together? That's where emotional resilience plays its part. Emotional resilience is your ability to relax a racing mind after a stressful situation. It is your built-in motivation to keep yourself in one piece whenever life throws something nasty your way.

You are born with emotional resilience and spend the rest of your life developing and strengthening it, but not everyone has the same level of resilience. This chapter will look at what it is, why yours might not be as strong as someone else's, and how to strengthen it.

Understanding Resilience

In today's fast-paced life, everyone is under pressure and faces stress, and this affects mental health and your ability to regulate your emotions, leading to the risk of burnout. You must be aware of your emotions. You must understand how any given situation makes you feel, and you must understand how to build up your emotional resilience. That's the only way you can understand those emotions and learn to adapt to whatever you have to face.

When you are emotionally resilient, you can cope with unexpected, potentially hostile situations and respond to them in the right way, returning to a calm state quickly afterward. It's not about your endurance levels in terms of stress; it's about how you bring yourself back together afterward.

You can build your emotional resilience in several ways, including regular physical exercise and mindfulness meditation to help support your emotional health.

Why You Need Emotional Resilience

Emotional regulation is a crucial skill to learn, but finding it when you are in an emotionally charged state is not easy. If you don't take some time out for yourself and learn to understand your emotions, your emotional resilience will be poor, making things worse for you.

When you develop strong emotional resilience, you understand how to respond to a challenge and how your emotions work. It gives you a better perspective of a situation, making it easier to respond healthily and not succumb to negative emotions.

Emotional Resilience Characteristics

It takes time to build your emotional resilience, and it's usually done by taking time for yourself. Walking in a peaceful nature setting, doing hobbies to enjoy, or meditating can all help build your resilience, but finding the time to do it isn't always easy.

The characteristics of good emotional resilience are:

- **Awareness of Your Mental Health:** When your emotional resilience is high, you are more aware of your positive and negative emotions. More importantly, you understand how they make you feel. You know your emotional triggers and how to wind down and recoup after a tough day. When a stressful situation arises, you know how to respond properly. Building that awareness is done best by using grounding techniques and mindfulness meditation.

- **Having a Support System:** Knowing you have a good support system in place is one of the most important parts of your mental health. Knowing you have someone you can lean on and talk to can ease your mind and make it easier for you to be more aware of your emotions. Humans have an innate need for connections, so build that support system today for better mental health tomorrow.

- **No Judgement:** Emotionally resilient people do not judge themselves like those with low resilience do. Many people refuse to acknowledge mental health issues, believing they are bad and not to be talked about or acknowledged at any cost. People with those thoughts tend to feel more inadequate and guilty, leading to poor emotional awareness. Emotional resilience makes you more aware of your mental health, allows you the time and space to understand it, and not judge yourself when you struggle with something, you accept things and move on.

- **More Positivity:** If you are emotionally resilient, you'll have a better view of life. You can usually see a good side to every situation, even the most stressful ones. You are more optimistic, making your emotional resilience much stronger.

- **More Confidence:** Similarly, someone with strong emotional resilience will look forward, confident that the stress will pass and things will improve. When you face an emotional situation, believing that your negative emotions will pass gives you the strength to carry on.

How to Develop a Resilient Mindset

How quickly do you bounce back from a setback? The stronger your emotional resilience, the better you will handle stress and the less chance of you lashing out. Resilient people have better stress management and are more positive.

Some people are naturally emotionally resilient, while others aren't. If you fall into the latter camp, don't worry. You can learn and build resilience with time, effort, and determination. Here are some ways to do it:

Find Your Sense of Purpose

This can help you see the meaning of any challenge you face. Rather than letting your problems set you back, you'll have the motivation to use past experiences as a learning curve and move forward. Some examples of how to do this are:

- Build a strong support system

- Improve your lifestyle

- Learn more about other cultures

- Make music or take up art

- Do something for your community

When you face an emotional situation, a sense of purpose is important in helping you bounce back. Anything you can do to give you that will help.

Believe You Can Do It

If you believe you can cope with a stressful situation, you will find it easier to do so. Self-confidence is important, especially confidence in coping and responding healthily to a situation. Learn to hear your inner voice and when it is talking negatively. When you hear it speak something negative, learn to replace it with a positive comment. When your inner voice says, "You can't do this," replace it with "I absolutely have this." If it tells you that you are useless at your job, replace it with "I am great at my job."

Self-esteem is one of the most important factors in facing challenges and recovering, so keep telling yourself that you've got this, that you are strong, and that you've achieved so much.

Build a Good Social Network

Everyone needs a strong support network, people they can talk to in times of need. It's one of the things that can help you be stronger, knowing you have someone to turn to. Being able to talk through a situation with someone close won't make the situation disappear, but it lets you air your feelings and get a better perspective on things. It gives you support and helps to come up with healthy solutions.

Learn to Embrace Change

A big part of emotional resilience is the ability to be flexible. Adaptability means you have a better chance of responding in the right way when a crisis hits. An emotionally resilient person often sees a crisis as an opportunity to move on to bigger and better things. Those who aren't so resilient may find that sudden changes flatten them, leaving them floundering. Being able to embrace change gives you more strength to fight back and thrive in any situation.

Ditch Pessimism for Optimism

Pessimism can drag you deeper into the depths when you face a bad situation. Learning to be more optimistic can help you become more resilient. Yes, you may be facing a tough time, but optimism shows you the way to the light at the end of the tunnel. Being optimistic doesn't mean you can push the problem aside. It means realizing that you will face setbacks throughout life but can cope with them, knowing better things lie ahead.

Look After Yourself

Stress can leave you feeling drained, and the temptation is to ignore your own needs. You might not be hungry, not feeling like going out for your daily walk, and you might nor sleep properly. These are common reactions to stress, but they do nothing to help your mental health. Take the time for self-care, even when you feel at your worst, and do things that make you happy. That will strengthen your mental resolve, resilience, and health and make you ready to face the world.

Learn Problem-Solving Skills

If you have good problem-solving skills, you can come up with good solutions when faced with a problem. That makes it easier for you to cope with stressful situations. You'll struggle to resolve issues if you don't have these skills. When you face a new situation, quickly list a few ways to resolve it. Try different things and work out the best way to work through issues. When you practice solving problems regularly, you will find it easier to cope when a really difficult situation arises.

Create Goals

It's not easy facing a situation that could be hostile. Sometimes, you'll feel like there's no way around a problem, no way to solve it. If you are emotionally resilient, you won't feel like that. You'll have a realistic view of the situation and be able to set good goals to deal with it. When faced with a situation, step back and assess what is happening. Come up with solutions and break each one down into smaller steps. You'll find it much easier to deal with the problem and, in the future, you'll be able to cope earlier and easier.

Do Something

If you sit back for an issue to go away, you'll be waiting a long time. All that happens is the problem gets worse. Instead, take action to solve things straight away. Don't expect a simple solution to every problem, but you can start taking steps to ease the situation and reduce the stress. Focus on what you have already done and work out your next steps. Don't let things discourage you. By working on resolving issues right from the start, you'll have more control over things.

Keep Working

Resilience can be built, but it takes time. If you still struggle to face certain situations, don't worry. Just keep on developing your resilience skills, and you will get to a stage where your coping skills are better and you are more emotionally resilient.

Overcoming Setbacks

Setbacks are a sad fact of life. You might have worked hard, but someone else got your promotion. Your boss tells you they don't like how you've been working. Anything can set you back, and rejection hurts. You might feel like giving up and walking away, but what does that solve?

Learning to recover from these setbacks makes you stronger in the long run. In fact, your whole life will be full of obstacles. Some you'll clear easily, while others will trip you up. Get used to it, but don't let the trips knock your confidence. The better you can pick yourself up and move on, the stronger your emotional resilience.

It might interest you to learn that some of the most successful people in the world have had their fair share of failures and setbacks:

- **Steven Spielberg:** He's made and directed so many of the world's most popular movies and won three Academy Awards, but the School of Cinematic Arts at the University of Southern California rejected him – twice!

- **Katy Perry:** Now an incredibly popular musical artist, it took her nine years and four record labels before success struck.

- **Walt Disney:** He was told he didn't have any good ideas and had no imagination by a former newspaper editor!

- **Oprah Winfrey:** She lost her first TV anchor job because she showed too much emotional investment in the stories.

Look where they are now! None of these people allowed the setbacks to stop them from doing what they wanted. When you fail at something, it should teach you how to get over the next obstacle. It should teach you to see where you need to improve and build your skills to succeed next time. And it should help you strengthen your resilience so that you can handle it next time you face an unexpected situation.

So, how do you strengthen your resilience so you can cope with setbacks?

Here's how.

- **Allow Yourself to Sulk – A Little**

People who tell you to get over things and move on have probably never faced a serious setback in their lives. You can't just get up and continue as if nothing happened. You need a little time to process what happened and you need time to feel a little sorry for yourself. Take whatever time you need, but don't let it drag on.

Do some meditation, spend the day watching your favorite Netflix shows, or do something that helps you clear your system. The important thing is not to let it pull you down so far that you struggle to bounce back. When you've had that time, get up and move forward.

- **Determine What the Setback Was**

Before you can do that, you must know what the setback was. What type was it?

- **A small bump in the road** – This just slows you a little, or stops you from doing what you need or want. It could be as simple as a team member falling ill, meaning an important project deadline is missed.

- **An obstacle** – A bit bigger, something that gets in your way. Perhaps you didn't get an interview for a job you really wanted, or you got the interview but not the job.

- **A serious event** – A serious illness or something unexpected and big- changes everything.

The type of setback determines how you react.

- **Accept You Can't Change Everything**

If your flight is delayed or you get stuck in a long traffic jam, does it ruin your whole day? Why? You can't change what's happened; it's not your fault, and you cannot control it. Allowing it to drag you down just wastes your time and energy and results in negative emotions, making you feel even worse. Your focus should be on things you do have control over and can take positive action for.

- **Have an Action Plan**

When you have a setback, you must be able to go at it with one thought in mind – not doing anything simply isn't an option. But don't rush into it. Have a plan so that your actions are filled with confidence.

Think about all your options. Could you change anything? What level of risk are you prepared to take? Let's say you didn't get an interview for that job you wanted. Your action plan would be along these lines:

- Look at your resume and job application
- Ask a trusted friend to have a look and give you feedback
- Call the recruiter and ask for their feedback.

Whatever your plan is, make sure every step is positive.

If you still find things overwhelming, focus on doing one small thing to get things moving. It's all about moving forward, however you do it.

- Don't Beat Yourself Up

Setbacks happen to everyone. Let's be fair; what would you learn if your whole life was easy and you had no stress? Not much! Setbacks allow you to learn creative thinking, learn who you really are, and what you can do. No one is perfect, so don't beat yourself up. Everyone has to figure stuff out in their lives, and so do you.

- Stop Blaming Others

Everyone needs a break, not just you. If someone lets you down or your plans don't come to fruition, slinging blame at others is easy. Stop because it's not helping you or anyone else. All it does is make you feel worse and stop you from learning from things and taking the right steps.

- Take Time for Reflection

Yes, you probably feel a little hurt and raw right now, but you must reflect on things. Looking back over an experience is a good way to learn how to respond and to become more emotionally resilient.

Sit and write what happened. Talk about it with someone else. Ask yourself – is there anything you could have done differently? Should you have done something else? Was there anything you should have noticed to prepare you for the setback? If yes, make sure you are better prepared next time. Determine how you can avoid the next one and overcome the obstacles in your way.

How you deal with one setback teaches you how to deal with another. You can do something, and you can come back stronger. Just take the time to build up your skills and learn to become more emotionally aware and resilient.

CHAPTER
SEVEN

Creating a Supportive Environment

Emotions are a part of your everyday life, especially your personal and professional relationships. They can strengthen or weaken your connections, which is why it's important to understand the impact emotions have on you and others. This chapter is all about how emotions influence your relationships and how to strengthen your connections with emotional regulation.

Emotional regulation is about how well you manage and control your emotions. You need to recognize your feelings and understand them or you cannot respond to them effectively or constructively. Better emotional regulation means being able to make good decisions and use effective communication to help strengthen your relationships.

The Impact of Emotions on Relationships

So, how do emotions impact your relationships? In several ways, to be honest:

1. **Communication:** Positive emotions make you a more effective communicator, while negative emotions have the opposite

effect. If you are upset or angry, you are more likely to lash out when faced with a tough situation, saying things you'll regret. This can cause conflict within a relationship. Conversely, when you are happy, your communication is happier and more effective, leading to stronger connections.

2. **Understanding and Empathy:** Emotions play a big part in this. When you understand your own emotions, you can understand other peoples'. This lets you respond in the right way, more empathetically, and provide the right support. When you validate another person's feelings, your environment is more supportive.

3. **Intimacy and Trust:** Negative emotions do not invite trust or intimacy into a relationship. However, when you can express your emotions healthily and positively, your relationships with strengthen and become more intimate and full of trust. It works the other way, too. If you feel that your partner hears your words and respects your feelings, you feel more connected and safer. If you shut down or get angry all the time, there's no room for that trust to grow.

4. **Conflict Resolution:** All relationships have setbacks, but your emotions can determine whether you can resolve or worsen them. You cannot resolve disagreements properly if you cannot regulate your emotions. Strengthen your emotional regulation, and you'll be much calmer when you face a tough situation.

5. **Emotional Support:** A good relationship has an excellent support system where both people get emotional support from each other. This support system requires that each party understands the other's emotions (and their own) and can validate them. Again, emotional regulation allows you to be empathetic and caring towards others, especially in tough situations, strengthening your connection and providing security.

Identifying Supportive vs. Toxic Relationships

While all relationships have their ups and downs, there is a world of difference between a healthy, supportive relationship and a toxic one.

If your relationship is healthy, you will be fully committed to resolving problems as they arise, using respect and compassion. In a toxic relationship, conflict may leave you feeling unsafe, and one or both of you will be unhappy and likely feel drained.

Healthy relationships provide loving, supportive connections, while unhealthy relationships can damage one or both of you and have a negative effect on your emotional, mental, and physical well-being. These relationships are usually marked by a lack of communication, trust, support and/or respect.

Understanding the difference is critical to helping you choose the right relationships in your life.

How to Have a Healthy Relationship

Healthy relationships revolve around a number of components, not least being able to express your emotions, needs, and boundaries and both of you treating the other as an equal. Cultivating these relationships involves:

- **Communication:** Effective communication is key because you must be able to be open and honest with your partner about your emotions and boundaries.

- **Trust:** Another crucial component is that both of you should fully trust each other.

- **Respect:** If you don't respect each other or you/their feelings and boundaries, your relationship is not healthy.

- **Support:** You should both provide support for each other financially, emotionally, and any other type of support needed.

- **Boundaries:** You must respect the boundaries each of you sets. This includes boundaries around making decisions, having space, and needing time.

- **Compromise:** Compromise is a healthy part of a good relationship, as it helps you resolve conflicts quicker and come back from them.

- **Time:** Each of you needs to make time for the other and put each other ahead of other things and people.

Your mental and physical health is important to keeping a healthy relationship. You must be willing to face challenges and resolve them and you can't do that if you are emotionally drained.

How to Tell a Healthy Relationship from a Toxic One

There are always signs that indicate whether a relationship is healthy or toxic.

Healthy Relationship:

- **Acceptance:** Both of you accept the other completely, flaws and all. To get to this stage, you must focus on the positives in each person and learn to have an open mind. Remember that, as time passes, people change, and you will likely not share all the same interests and values, nor will you have the same goals.

- **Independence:** Yes, you must be there for one another but you also need your independence. Both parties should be allowed to have interests and friends that don't come into the relationship, and both should be encouraged to do their own thing at times and respect the other's desire to be alone.

- **Honesty:** You should be honest and open with one another and be able to discuss your feelings without judgment or repercussions. You should also never keep secrets from one another.

- **Emotional Intimacy:** You must be able to talk about your deepest feelings and have an emotional connection with each other. You can get to this stage by making time to have deep, intimate conversations about your feelings and being honest about them.

- **Equal Power:** No one person should be above the other in a relationship and no one should be made to feel small and powerless. In a healthy relationship, both of you share the decision-making, especially those that revolve around both of you. And neither person tries to dominate or control the other.

- **Full Support:** You both support each other and encourage each other to reach for your dreams and work toward your goals. You must be encouraging and prepared to help each other when needed.

Any relationship with those qualities is positive and healthy. However, remember that everyone is different, and no two relationships are the same – everyone faces challenges. To build a healthy relationship, be it personal or professional, you must focus on building trust, be honest and open, and respect the other person.

Unhealthy Relationship:

- **No Communication:** Unhealthy relationships are usually characterized by a serious lack of communication between you. One or both of you could struggle to open up or set boundaries, which can lead to resentment.

- **No Trust:** There will also likely be little to no trust between you, and at least one party in the relationship has probably lied, been unfaithful, or done something else to lose the trust of the other person. This can lead to insecurity.

- **No Respect:** One of you doesn't respect the other or both of you have no respect for each other. You take no notice of each other's thoughts, feelings, and boundaries, which can lead to hurt and disrespect.

- **No Support:** One or both may feel the other doesn't support them enough, leaving you feeling isolated and lonely.

- **No Boundaries:** If one or both of you have no boundaries or cross those set by the other, it leads to resentment. You should both respect boundaries and give each other time and space when needed.

- **Unhealthy Conflict Resolution:** You may resort to unhealthy mechanisms to try and resolve conflicts, such as screaming, throwing things, name-calling, and even getting physically violent with one another.

Relationships with these traits are unhealthy, and one or both of you must seek the support of a trusted friend or therapist to fix what's gone wrong. If the relationship is beyond repair, be prepared to walk away – and find somewhere safe if necessary.

Building a Support Network

Have you ever moved somewhere different or started a new job and wondered how you would make those all-important connections? It's not easy to build new relationships, but, as said before, humans need connections to make their lives meaningful.

It doesn't matter whether its chatting to a stranger or meeting new people at work or on social media. You need social skills to build those relationships and create networks, but it's not just about being social. It's also about your professional and personal growth.

Sadly, not everyone wants to join in, making things a bit uncomfortable to start with. Even more so if you have social anxiety and really struggle to connect with others. It may sound counter-intuitive, but to learn to connect with people, you need to be comfortable with your feelings of awkwardness and discomfort.

It's worth the effort, especially if you build some meaningful relationships and a great support network. Here's why making connections with others is so important and some great ways you can try to get started.

Learn to Understand Yourself

The COVID-19 pandemic taught us that friendships and connections are more important than ever before. Many people develop much deeper connections with others, which can be valuable. They teach you that there's nothing wrong with vulnerability and that asking for help when you need it is definitely wrong.

Meaningful relationships grow from strong connections. Research has also shown that exercise isn't the only thing that can boost your health – good social connections can, too. When you have good connections with others, your mental health is better, your mood improves, your blood pressure lowers, and you can even extend your life.

However, not everyone finds it easy to connect with others. Some people don't have enough self-confidence, are shy, and are anxious about meeting people. This can stop them from putting themselves in a situation where they can meet new people. At the same time, if they lack self-esteem or have poor mental health, they won't even try to connect, even when they do meet people.

Some people also find it hard to ask questions, which is one of the best ways to start a conversation. You'll struggle to connect if your questions don't promote interesting conversation. Luckily, you can learn this skill.

Top Ways to Help You Build Connections

Sometimes, it's easy to connect, while other times it won't. For example, if you find yourself working with someone you went to college with, you've got something in common and can connect easily. You'll also find connecting with people who share your hobbies and interests easier.

That said, making an instant connection doesn't automatically lead to a strong relationship. You should never put any connection under that sort of pressure. Sure, a friendship may follow, but loose connections are just as important in some ways as strong ones; they make life a little more interesting for a start.

Sometimes, you'll need to work harder to make a connection. You've probably realized throughout life that most of your friendships take time to build. Let's say that you share a table in your work's canteen with someone from another department. Neither of you understands the other person's job, and you don't really have anything in common, but over time, you've had some great conversations and are gradually beginning to connect. Think back, and you'll probably see that some of your strongest friendships have been built in this way. To build a good connection, you need two things: social skills and an open mind.

Learning to connect with others is actually easier than you realize:

1. Be Yourself

You honestly cannot go wrong by being yourself. Trying to be someone you aren't is a recipe for disaster, and it just leads to relationships based on lies. When you start to feel more comfortable with yourself later on, it will lead to confusion in the relationship. If someone desperately wants to fit in, pretending to be someone else is easier, but being yourself is the only way to make real connections. Yes, you might feel vulnerable to start with, but you will gradually feel more secure.

2. Respect Boundaries

Getting to know someone will soon teach you what their limits are. For example, if you chat with your nearest colleague, it might become apparent that they don't like discussing their personal life. Respect that. Don't keep trying to get them to talk about it, or you will destroy their trust and your connection.

You should try to talk about things other than just work, though. If the other party is okay with it, try deepening your conversations. Ask about their interests, their aspirations, and anything that doesn't cross their lines. If you show you are willing to open up, they may eventually become comfortable with sharing more with you.

3. Stay in the Present

If you are talking to someone, make sure your focus is on them. Forget about your phone, stop thinking about your plans for the weekend, and focus 100% on the present. That's the best way to connect – others will know if your focus has wandered. And it's not just about your mind being present. Your body language should show it, too. If you are turned away from the person you are talking to, they'll know your attention is not on them and know you have no interest in making a connection.

4. Get Past the Surface

A deep connection goes way beyond small talk. That's fine the first couple of times you talk, but you need to start taking things further. Ask them about their goals, values, and hopes for the future. Asking these questions helps you learn who they are and shows them that you are interested in creating a deeper connection.

5. Share Your Conversation

Two people talking should have a back-and-forth conversation, and there should be plenty of give and take. For example, if you are talking to someone about their long-term plans, they should ask you what yours are. If they don't, it could just be they got distracted – although that shouldn't happen. If you feel like the conversation is one-sided, don't hesitate to step in and offer your stories and information. If their attention is still on them, it's probably wise to walk away and forget about making the connection.

6. Show Genuine Appreciation

Be careful with your compliments. Well-placed, genuine appreciation is usually well-received, and it can lead to much deeper connections and relationships. Compliments for the sale of giving them or because you are trying to curry favor won't get you anywhere. In fact, shallow compliments just lead to a lack of trust.

7. Show You Can Listen

Being an active listener can tell you quite a lot about the person speaking. Think back on conversations you have had. Do you tend to interrupt when they are talking? Do you judge them? Having an open mind and listening attentively while someone speaks allows you to get to know them better. It also means not having to repeat a question because you weren't listening to the answer or asking them to say something again.

People like to know that you are listening when they speak, and it's one of the best ways to make good connections.

8. Make Time to Connect

Everyone has busy times, making it feel like there's no time for anything, let alone connecting with others. If you struggle with organization, find a way to schedule time into your busy day. Look at what's coming up on your calendar and find a time when you can be more social and connect with others. Do weekends work best for you? Evenings? Whenever it is, schedule some time and stick to it.

9. Keep Eye Contact

Eye contact is, hands down, the easiest way to show someone you are listening and interested. It helps the other person see that you want to make that connection and tells them you are happy to be there and don't want to be elsewhere. Eye contact shows trust. It keeps a conversation open and honest and helps keep things going. However, there is such a thing as too much eye contact. Don't stare at a person, as it can make them feel uncomfortable. Just be natural and use the right amount to keep the conversation flowing.

10. Smile

You can't always see what is happening beneath the surface, and you may be talking to someone socially anxious. The conversation could be very hard for them and is a way for them to learn. When you meet them and throughout the conversation, smile – but make it genuine, not forced. It can help reduce stress and make the conversation less awkward for both people. Smiles are positive and help make people feel comfortable.

How to Build Deeper Connections

If you are genuinely interested in deepening a connection, don't be afraid to get curious – but don't be nosy. Ask questions that help them open up, listen actively, and maintain eye contact. Show them that you are present and enjoying the conversation. Find common ground, but don't forget to share things about yourself as well. Read their body language, make sure yours is positive, and respect their boundaries. Practice makes perfect and allows you to build much stronger connections and a great support network.

Seeking Professional Help

If your emotions consistently get the better of you, and you can't control them, regardless of what you try, it might be time to seek professional help. You might have considered seeing a therapist but balked at the last minute. You might have convinced yourself you don't really need one or that the problem will pass if you just wait.

Knowing the right time to see a therapist is not easy. Everyone has off days, and most people go through a bad patch in their lives, but you must understand when the time is right to get the help you need. Here are some reasons why seeing a therapist can benefit you:

- **You Struggle with Mental Health**

Life is challenging and you may be finding it hard to balance everything you have to do. Stress rises, you struggle to manage your feelings and you certainly can't process them. It's more likely that you are not using the most effective methods to manage your stress, and a therapist can help you separate everything and work through your emotions. They can also give you the tools you need to manage them.

- **You Can't Manage Stress**

Life is full of stress, and there's no way to eliminate it all. To be fair, a certain amount of stress can benefit you. However, if it gets too much for you and you struggle to manage it, you may need to consider seeing a therapist. Unmanaged stress can cause all sorts of issues, not least fraying tempers, irritability, and inefficiency. A therapist can teach you how to manage stress and solve problems to eliminate some of the stress in your life.

- **You Can't Regulate Your Emotions**

Sometimes, it's a struggle to handle emotions, especially when they are tough ones, like anger and anxiety. If strong emotions seem to control you, you can get help by talking to a therapist. They can teach you anger and stress management techniques or some reduction strategies to help you manage those emotions better. They can also help you figure out what's behind it all.

- **You Have Unhealthy Coping Skills**

Stress can make you turn to unhealthy ways to manage it, such as drinking, smoking, or overeating. These don't solve anything; they merely bring added problems and make you feel worse. It's worth remembering that few coping skills are healthy. Some people spend days lying in bed or watching TV just to take their mind off things. Anything you use to cope with your stress and anxiety can be bad if you overuse them, or that's the only reason you do them. By turning to these, you are not facing your problems. A therapist can help you learn healthier skills to manage and cope with your emotions while also helping you deal with the problem.

Other Reasons to See a Therapist

Therapists don't just help you deal with stress and anxiety. They can also help you improve your relationships and self.

- **You Want Better Relationships**

If you struggle with relationships, know that there are many reasons why this might be. It could be a lack of assertiveness, fear of conflict, inability to get close to someone, and many other reasons. A therapist can help you get to the root of the problem and determine what's stopping you from having good relationships. They'll give you the tools and skills to form and keep good connections.

- **You Want Better Self-Awareness**

Have you done things that make you stop and wonder why? Perhaps you broke up your relationship, even though your partner seemed like the right person. Perhaps you responded inappropriately to something because nerves got the better of you. Much of this is down to a lack of self-awareness, and a therapist can help you understand why you behave the way you do. They can help you find relationship patterns or thinking patterns in your life and any self-limiting beliefs that stop you from moving forward. Whatever lies at the bottom of it, a therapist can help you find it and learn to deal with it.

- **You Need Help to Cope With a Major Transition**

Perhaps you have moved to a completely different area, got a new job, had a child, or even ended a long-term relationship. No matter what it is, you might be struggling to cope with the emotions that arise. A therapist can help you talk through everything and provide you with emotional support while teaching you skills to help you cope and adapt.

- **Your Mood Is Affecting Your Colleagues and Work**

Everyone feels down sometimes, but if your mood is affecting your productivity and your relationships with colleagues, it's time to get some help. A therapist can help you get past what's bringing you down. They can help you recognize the sticking points and teach you how to process and manage your emotions and change how you think.

- **Your Mood Is Affecting Your Sleep and Appetite**

You may not realize you are stressed or that you are a bit snappy or off. You will notice if your appetite suddenly changes and you struggle to sleep properly. Some people struggle with emotions to the extent that their appetite goes, while others turn to food – usually unhealthy choices – to help them cope. Some people find they can't sleep properly, while others just want to sleep all the time. You might sleep for the same number of hours as normal but will feel unusually tired because your sleep hasn't been the best quality. Whatever the effect, a therapist can help you determine what's going on with your emotions. You should also see a doctor to make sure your sleep and appetite problems aren't down to another cause.

- **You No Longer Have an Interest in Your Hobbies**

This might sound like a daft reason to see a therapist, but there are often emotional reasons behind a sudden change like this. If you used to love gardening or going for long walks and suddenly find you have no interest anymore, it usually indicates something isn't quite right. Yes, people lose interest in things, but if you no longer want to do anything, it's time to find out what happened. The same thing applies to your social life. If you suddenly stop wanting contact with others, there's usually something else at play. You could be depressed or anxious but not realize it. With the help of a therapist, you can determine what's causing the problem and how to manage it.

There are many more reasons why you might need to consider a therapist, but mainly, it will come down to your emotions and your inability to process and manage them.

How to Find a Therapist

In early times, you wouldn't seek any help unless you were actually sick, and some insurance companies wouldn't pay out unless you were receiving treatment for an existing illness, such as anxiety or depression. These days, people have more awareness of mental health and find it much easier to talk about. And you don't have to wait until the problem has gotten out of hand before you seek help. In fact, you can use a therapist to help you prevent things from getting bad.

1. What Kind of Therapist Do You Need?

When you are trying to treat a mental health condition or issue, you will need to consider exactly what you need. Your first port of call should always be your doctor, as some physical conditions can mimic mental health issues. If there's nothing wrong with you physically, ask them to refer you to a therapist.

If it's your emotions, thinking patterns, and behaviors you need help with, you'll need one who specializes in your condition – they aren't all the same, and some specialize in mental health.

2. Get Some Referrals

Do you have health insurance? In that case, ring your insurer and ask them for the contact details of regional therapists who will accept your insurance. You want three or four at least, just in case you can't get in with the first one. You should also clarify with your insurer exactly what they cover. If you don't have insurance, try your local mental health community center – you'll find their number in the phone book.

3. Time to Call

Pick up the phone. This is one of the hardest parts because it means you have to admit to yourself – and sometimes others – that you have a problem. If you can't do it, ask a trusted friend to do it for you. Make the appointment and make sure they know it's your first time. That way, they can make sure you have enough time for plenty of talking. If they tell you that you have to wait several months, make the appointment and then move on to the other numbers. It's easier to cancel appointments than get them, so you're covered if someone comes up who can see you much quicker. You should also get your name on the list for people to call when an appointment is canceled. Just be aware that you may be expected to attend an appointment at short notice.

4. Ask the Questions

You'll be looking for advice on your first appointment, so don't be afraid to ask questions. Tell them that you want a therapist you can work with over the long term.

- Do they make you feel comfortable? They may be the most highly qualified therapist and have a great reputation, but that doesn't mean you'll get on! You will be asked a lot of personal questions during your sessions that could bring up feelings of discomfort. Only the questions should do that, not the therapist, so if you don't get a good vibe, look for another one.

- Find out their educational level and how much professional experience they have.

- Find out if they have worked with people with similar issues to yours? How long for?

- Ask how you can work together to solve your problems.

- Ask how often you will meet, for how long, and how easy getting an appointment will be. Can you email or call them in between?

- Ask how they and you gauge your improvements.

You need to ask any questions that will help you gauge the therapist and whether they are right for you, so think about what to ask before you go to the appointment.

5. Build Your Relationship

You might feel that your therapist isn't right for you on the first visit, so just move on and find another one. You have to make the right choice. Your therapist is part of your support network, and they may be with you for some time. You need one who listens, considers your perspective, and works with you to teach you how to cope and manage your emotions.

There is no shame in going to a therapist, and it doesn't mean you are weak. It also doesn't mean you have something wrong with you. It just means that you want to become a better you; there's nothing wrong with that. You are not weak – you are stronger than you know simply by admitting that you need a bit of help.

CHAPTER

EIGHT

Practical Applications in Daily Life

L ife is full of surprises, some of them not as exciting as others. And with all the twisting and turning, it's easy to get dragged along for the ride, forgetting to look after your well-being. Good emotional health is critical for a healthy life and there are some things you can do every day to strengthen yours.

Integrating Emotional Management into Your Routine

The following practices should be done daily to help you strengthen your emotional awareness.

1. **Practice Gratitude:** Take the time to think about everything you are grateful for. It could be the sunrise or sunset, your family, friends, or anything that makes you feel happy and contented.

2. **Mindful Breathing:** Do deep breathing exercises every day. Close your eyes and breathe in and out deeply, focusing on how it feels when the air goes into your lungs and then leaves. This can help you cut your stress levels, make you more self-aware, and help you relax.

3. **Keep Moving:** Physical activity benefits your mental and emotional health as much as your physical. Make time for daily physical activity, even if it's just a brisk walk around the block. Find activities you enjoy and build them into your life.

4. **Connect with Other People:** Connecting with others is a great way to boost your mental and emotional health. Build and maintain strong connections with family, friends, and community members. Whether it's time for a coffee or a day out, make sure you spend time with people who make you happy.

5. **Keep Screen Time to a Minimum:** Most people are glued to a screen – TV, tablet, phone, computer, etc. The more you use one, the easier it is to succumb to the mental stimulation it provides, making it harder for you to relax. It can also interfere with your sleep. Set a limit on your screen time, especially in the evenings, and find other activities that feed your emotional health – reading, an evening with friends, a hobby, etc.

6. **Learn Compassion:** For yourself as well as others. Self-compassion means being kind to yourself, especially when you face tough times. Treat yourself as you would treat a friend in the same situation.

7. **Get Enough Sleep:** Good quality sleep is one of the most important factors in your emotional health. It doesn't matter how long you sleep, so long as you get good, restful sleep and don't walk up exhausted. Rather than criticizing yourself and

beating yourself up, put your energies into doing things that help you sleep well.

8. **Practice Mindfulness:** Mindfulness helps you stay fully aware of the present moment. Mindfulness meditation is an excellent way to help you do this, so find a few minutes daily to practice, and you'll find it easier to manage stress, reduce anxiety, and feel better overall.

9. **Feed Your Body:** A healthy diet feeds your body and mind, so choose nutrient-rich whole foods over processed and junk foods, and drink plenty of water.

10. **Get Spiritual:** It doesn't matter whether you choose meditation, prayer, or getting out in nature. Spiritual practices can help you find your sense of purpose and give your life a deeper meaning.

You don't have to do everything on this list, certainly not every day. Choose one or two that resonate with you and stick with those first. You might find that certain practices work better for different things, and some will fit into your schedule better. So long as you make time to do something every day, you can start to strengthen your emotional health to manage and process your feelings much better.

Using Emotions as a Guide

A lot of people think that emotions should never be involved when it comes to decision-making and believe that, in fact, they would be better off if they just pushed their emotions to one side and ignored them altogether. Rather than process their feelings and understand what caused them, they suppress them, believing rationality is far better than being emotional.

The truth is that emotions are a valuable tool, especially in making decisions. Without them, you wouldn't have any motivation. You would sit back and wouldn't do a thing. Your emotions inform your decisions because that's what they are for. Emotions can make a situation clearer, helping you evaluate it and make the right decision to respond quickly and effectively.

Your emotions are driven by one this – your innate need to survive. Although they are there to direct you, their messages are usually submitted way below any conscious awareness. And because they are there for your survival, they are fast, which means you can't always trust them to direct you the right way. Emotions are not particularly detailed or specific, but they are effective. This is why your emotions may not always be the right ones in a certain situation, and that's why you need to ensure your response is appropriate at any given time.

Using Your Emotions to Make Decisions

The following steps will help you use your emotions effectively to make decisions:

- **Welcome Them:** Don't push your emotions aside and ignore them. Identify them, understand them, and recognize how they make you feel. Try to understand why. This self-examination is mindful and helps you make the best decisions for any situation.

- **Don't Forget Emotional Bias:** Emotions are a survival feature, which means they act fast and don't always provide the right information. The emotional brain isn't as bothered about being right as it is about being safe. Listen to your emotions, but question them before you act.

- **Learn Emotional Regulation:** Intense emotions can get in the way of rational thinking and damage your judgment. That makes critical thinking and objectivity difficult. This is why you need to learn how to regulate your emotions and tamp them down a little to make the right decision for a situation.

- **Use Your Emotions to Guide You:** They are your compass. They point you in the right direction but should never be allowed to dictate to you. Try to get a balance between logical reason and emotional insight.

- **Use Your Rational Mind:** When you can do this, you can use the unconscious, intuitive, fast-thinking emotional system to guide you in making decisions in a slower, rational, more controlled, and conscious decision. This takes you from being irrational and impulsive to being flexible, rational, and strategic.

- **Think About the Context:** Every situation has a context, so you need to evaluate things, as that context can influence your emotions. When your emotions result from something that happened to you in the past or some kind of bias, it can affect how you judge things. Keep things in perspective, consider the context, and focus only on what's relevant.

- **Get the Information Together:** While the insights you get from your emotions are valuable, you should never take them as they are. Always use facts to back them up. Take some time to get the information you need before you make a decision. That way, providing you have considered everything, you are more likely to make the right decision,

- **Be Mindful:** Mindfulness helps calm and balance the mind. If your mind isn't regulated, it can come up with all sorts of delusions, and it will allow unchecked emotions free rein. When you are mindful, your emotions are clearer, and you can bring your rational mind into play.

- **Be Compassionate:** Having compassion when you make decisions is a good way of ensuring your decisions are ethical, filled with empathy, and balanced. That way, the well-being of everyone involved is considered. Compassion also helps calm your emotions and helps you make decisions that benefit everyone.

- **Learn Emotional Intelligence:** When you are emotionally intelligent, you can better recognize your emotions. That makes it easier for you to learn how to manage them. Emotional intelligence comprises self-regulation, social skills, self-awareness, empathy, and motivation. All of this helps you use your emotions to make better decisions rather than letting your emotions control you.

- **Change How You Think:** In any situation, you must reframe things. This means consciously changing how you think about the situation, thus controlling negative feelings. Do this by having compassion and empathy, not just for you but for everyone involved in the situation.

- **Widen Your Perspective:** See the bigger picture. You'll find that impulses and small things no longer get in your way when you can do that. Work out your long-term goals and work towards them to help you use your emotions for harmony and peace. It also lets you see that value-driven decisions offer a better outcome than those driven by emotions.

Emotions can and should be used when you make decisions, but you shouldn't let them control your every move. Use them right, and your decisions will be far more effective and will work for everyone. A combination of rational thinking and emotional insight helps you make well-rounded choices without letting your emotions run roughshod over everyone and everything.

Setting Goals for Emotional Growth

Emotional growth doesn't happen overnight. It takes time, effort, patience, and practice, and the best way to succeed is to draw up an emotional development plan. This involves the following four steps:

1. Work Out Your Strengths and Weaknesses

This is the first step in any personal development plan, not just one for emotional growth. Do this in whatever way makes sense: online quizzes, from others, giving you feedback, self-reflection, even a professional assessment. You want an honest, clear picture of where you are now and what areas need improvement. For example, time management and prioritization may be things you are strong at, but you may struggle to handle conflict or stressful situations – those are your weaknesses.

2. Determine Your Goals and How to Reach Them

Next, you need to work out your goals based on your weaknesses. Make sure they are SMART:

- **Specific:** Your goal must state exactly what you will do

- **Measurable:** It must state how you will measure your progress to keep yourself accountable

- **Achievable:** Set reasonable goals you can achieve rather than something you will struggle with

- **Relevant:** It must relate to what you want to achieve overall

- **Time-Bound:** It must have a timeline for you to complete it.

For example, let's say you want to reduce stress. You might say your goal is to reduce your stress levels by 25% within three months by learning emotional awareness and management techniques. The emotional awareness and management techniques could also be made into SMART

GOALS – it's all part of the bigger picture. Don't forget to list all the ways you will lower your stress levels.

3. Monitor Progress

It's no good setting a goal if you aren't going to monitor how you get on and whether you achieve it. Review your development plan weekly and note everything you have done towards the goal. That way, you can monitor your results, too. You can also use checklists, a journal, apps, or anything that helps you monitor your results. The idea is to evaluate what you have achieved. You should learn from any mistakes you make and celebrate your wins. For example, you could keep a record of whenever you get stressed, the feedback you get from other people, or how you manage situations.

4. Be Prepared to Adjust Things

Don't be afraid to change your plan and what you need to do to ensure your emotional intelligence grows. If you set a goal that makes your emotions worse, change it. If something isn't working, change it. When you do that, change your development plan so you always know exactly what you need to do. The idea is to improve continuously, not go backward. For example, your original goal of reducing your stress by 25% in three months may need to be adjusted to six months. Or you might need to add new goals or actions. Whatever it is, do it – your plan has to work for you and if it isn't working, it isn't right.

Conclusion

Thank you for reading this guide. It's hoped that it's given you an insight into your emotions and taught you some techniques to help you get a handle on them and how to control them.

Everyone faces situations that evoke certain emotions in them. Rather than avoiding those situations – which means avoiding life and people – you need to learn how to control your emotions and reactions. The wrong or extreme reaction will harm your ability to get on with others. Emotional regulation helps you:

- Face difficult situations and deal with them reasonably.

- Identify and deal with your emotions properly.

- Learn to control emotion instead of it controlling you.

- React in the right way to potentially dangerous situations.

- Increase your self-esteem.

- Feel more secure.

- Make your interpersonal relationships stronger.

What Is Emotional Control?

When you come up against a certain situation, it triggers a specific emotion. There are three components to the emotional regulatory process:

- Initiate an action

- Inhibit an action

- Modulate your response

You can think of emotional control as being a modifier, helping you understand crucial information about a situation and respond to it positively. Your feelings and emotional interpretation affect your thinking, how you make decisions, and go about your daily life. People who control their emotions are likelier to have better judgment skills and be more balanced than those who don't. That means they control their actions and can better judge the situation they face.

A lack of emotional control has also been shown to be linked to depression, anxiety, and some other mental health conditions. The more anxiety you have, the less control you have over your emotions.

How to Practice Better Control

Instead of focusing only on your emotions and reactions, learn to reflect on the situation. You can do this with practices like the following:

- Learning self-awareness

- Mindfulness

- Changing how you think

- Learning to be more flexible

- Adapting to change with coping mechanisms that work for you

- Having an emotional support network

- Learning self-compassion and positivity

Encouragement for Continued Growth

Learning emotional control and regulation is not a one-off. It's a continual learning process, and in the fast-paced world we live in now, it has become more important than ever before. Self-care and self-compassion are two of the most important tools in your arsenal, and both are equally important.

Self-care is all about being intentional in anything you do to improve your well-being, both physically and mentally and emotionally. Too many people see self-care as selfish or self-indulgent, but it is actually a way of helping you be the best you can be. When you neglect self-care, it leads to poor mental health and more chance of stress, and you are less likely to face challenges head-on.

Self-compassion is all about being kind to yourself, practicing acceptance, and understanding yourself, especially when you doubt yourself or feel you have failed. Rather than telling yourself off for a perceived mistake, self-compassion helps you be kind to yourself and learn to increase your self-esteem.

Self-compassionate people are less likely to be anxious, depressed, or stressed and are more likely to feel good about themselves and life. It can also boost your mental health by helping you have a more positive mindset.

Here's how these two important tools help your mental health:

- **Less Stress:** Self-care, such as meditation, hobbies, or exercise, can reduce stress and help you feel better.

- **Emotional Regulation:** Self-compassion helps you accept how you feel without judgment and that makes you feel better about yourself and make better decisions.

- **More Resilient:** Self-compassion and self-care can both help you face challenges and setbacks, increase your resilience and become mentally stronger.

- **Better Self-Esteem:** When you are kind to yourself, you see yourself more positively and learn to accept yourself, increasing self-esteem.

So, how do you incorporate these into your daily life?

1. **Put Your Needs First:** Recognizing and prioritizing your needs, regardless of how busy you are, is important. You must take time for yourself, even if it's just five minutes a day or a morning off one day a week. Use that time to do something that makes you happy.

2. **Consider Inner Dialog:** Consider your inner dialog, especially when you face a challenge. Be kind to yourself instead of telling

yourself off for something you did or didn't do or say. When you do, you'll find your emotional well-being improves.

3. **Practice Gratitude:** This is one of the most powerful self-care and self-compassion tools you have. Take a bit of time out each day to think about what you are grateful for. It can be the smallest thing, but it will help you refocus on positivity.

4. **Practice Self-Care:** How you do this is down to you; it's all about knowing what works for you and making time to do it regularly. It could be as simple as reading, going for a walk, or relaxing in a bath. Whatever helps you relax and feel good, do it.

5. **Find Support:** This final point is critical. Everyone needs help and support; you should never be afraid to ask for it. Be it a colleague, your partner, or a family member, or even joining a mental health support group or seeing a therapist, you should reach out when you need help.

Making self-care and self-compassion a daily habit is just as crucial, but it will take time. However, it is well worth it, so here are a few ways to help you:

- **Small Changes:** Choose and incorporate one or two practices into your life. From there, you can build up.

- **Consistency:** Doing these things once won't cut it; you need to make them a regular part of your life. It doesn't matter how busy you are; you must always make time for yourself.

- **Patience:** It takes time to make something a habit, so have patience and, whenever you score a victory, celebrate.

- **Track it:** Note your progress on an app or in a journal. That's the only way to keep your motivation levels high and be accountable.

Emotional regulation is an important skill to learn and self-care and self-compassion can both help you in your journey. The kinder you are to yourself, the better your mental health and emotional well-being.

You are not expected to read this book once and be completely in control of your emotions. You are in this for the long haul, for life, so take this guide one chapter at a time and put everything you learn into practice before you move on. Be kind to yourself and others, and you'll soon find that you control your emotions, not vice versa.

References

10 Daily Habits to Improve Your Emotional Well-Being \n \r\n. (2022). Friendsofash.org. https://www.friendsofash.org/10-daily-habits-to-improve-your-emotional-well-being

A Guided Meditation to Label Difficult Emotions. (2019, January 23). Mindful. https://www.mindful.org/a-guided-meditation-to-label-difficult-emotions/

Ackerman, C. (2019, July 10). *What are Positive and Negative Emotions and Do We Need Both?* PositivePsychology.com. https://positivepsychology.com/positive-negative-emotions/

Building Resilience: How to Bounce Back from Setbacks. (n.d.). Maxme - We Maximise Human Potential. https://www.maxme.com.au/insights/building-resilience-how-to-bounce-back-from-setbacks

Caba. (2024). *How to Talk About Your Feelings.* Caba.org.uk. https://www.caba.org.uk/your-health/your-mental-health/managing-mental-health/how-talk-feelings.html

Cherry, K. (2020, May 17). *The Purpose of Emotions.* Verywell Mind; Verywellmind. https://www.verywellmind.com/the-purpose-of-emotions-2795181

Conflict Resolution Skills - HelpGuide.org. (2018, November 3). HelpGuide.org.

https://www.helpguide.org/relationships/communication/conflict-resolution-skills

Davis, T. (2024, February 19). *A Step-by-Step Guide to Navigating Difficult Conversations*. Training. https://trainingmag.com/a-step-by-step-guide-to-navigating-difficult-conversations/

Emotional intelligence: Components, Importance, and Examples. (2022, May 30). Www.medicalnewstoday.com. https://www.medicalnewstoday.com/articles/components-of-emotional-intelligence#how-to-improve

Emotional Resilience. (n.d.). Health Assured. https://www.healthassured.org/blog/emotional-resilience/

Emotional Resilience: How to Build Emotional Resilience - 2024 - MasterClass. (2020). MasterClass. https://www.masterclass.com/articles/emotional-resilience

Grounding & Breathing Exercises for Calming Your Nervous System / Counseling & Psych Services (CAPS). (n.d.). Caps.arizona.edu. https://caps.arizona.edu/grounding

Harvard Health Publishing. (2019). *Six Relaxation Techniques to Reduce Stress -Harvard Health*. Harvard Health; Harvard Health. https://www.health.harvard.edu/mind-and-mood/six-relaxation-techniques-to-reduce-stress

Here's Why Emotional Intelligence Is So Important. (n.d.). Calm Blog. https://www.calm.com/blog/why-is-emotional-intelligence-important

Honest, Not Bossy: How to Assertive Communication. (2020, August 20). Healthline. https://www.healthline.com/health/assertive-communication#challenges

How to Know When It's Time to See a Therapist. (n.d.). Verywell Mind. https://www.verywellmind.com/how-to-know-when-it-s-time-to-see-a-therapist-5077040

How to Recognize the Causes of Stress. (n.d.). Healthline. https://www.healthline.com/health/stress-causes#how-to-cope

Importance of Expressing Your Emotions - Bayridge Counselling. (2022, October 12). Bayridge -. https://bayridgecounsellingcentres.ca/blog/importance-of-expressing-your-emotions/

Jones, K. (2024, July). *Emotions Play a Significant Role in Our Relationships. They can either strengthen or weaken the connection we have with others.* Linkedin.com. https://www.linkedin.com/pulse/impact-emotions-relationships-kim-jones-qqvfc

Khan, N. (2018, February 11). *What Are Primary And Secondary Emotions | Betterhelp.* Betterhelp.com; BetterHelp. https://www.betterhelp.com/advice/general/what-are-primary-and-secondary-emotions/

Ratson, M. (2023, August 7). *The Power of Emotions in Decision Making | Psychology Today.* Www.psychologytoday.com. https://www.psychologytoday.com/intl/blog/the-wisdom-of-anger/202308/the-power-of-emotions-in-decision-making

Schenck, L. K. (2011, June 18). *Recognize Your Emotions in 6 Steps - Mindfulness Muse.* Mindfulness Muse. https://www.mindfulnessmuse.com/dialectical-behavior-therapy/recognize-your-emotions-in-6-steps

Segal, J., Smith, M., Robinson, L., & Boose, G. (2018, November 3). *Body Language and Nonverbal Communication.* HelpGuide.org.

https://www.helpguide.org/relationships/communication/nonverbal-communication

The 8 Myths About Emotions That Are Holding Us Back – Amy Morin, LCSW. (2024). Amymorinlcsw.com. https://amymorinlcsw.com/the-8-myths-about-emotions-that-are-holding-us-back/

Tull, M. (2022, June 24). *How Cognitive-Behavioral Techniques Can Help People with PTSD.* Verywell Mind. https://www.verywellmind.com/cognitive-behavioral-coping-strategies-2797612

Wilkinson, J. (2020, October 28). *The Benefits of Regulating Your Emotions.* Wellspace Counseling. https://www.wellspacepdx.com/post/the-benefits-of-regulating-your-emotions

Wooll, M. (2022, June 1). *How to Connect With People: 10 Surefire Ways.* Www.betterup.com. https://www.betterup.com/blog/how-to-connect-with-people

Wright, K. W. (2023, June 21). *Emotional Journaling: How to Use Journaling to Process Emotions.* Day One | Your Journal for Life. https://dayoneapp.com/blog/emotional-journaling/

Made in the USA
Coppell, TX
28 February 2025

46516344R00090